The Most Famous Cities of the Maya: The Mayapán, and U

By Jesse Harasta and Char

Picture of El Castillo in Chichén Itzá, taken by Daniel Schwen

About Charles River Editors

Charles River Editors is a boutique digital publishing company, specializing in bringing history back to life with educational and engaging books on a wide range of topics. Keep up to date with our new and free offerings with this 5 second sign up on our weekly mailing list, and visit Our Kindle Author Page to see other recently published Kindle titles.

We make these books for you and always want to know our readers' opinions, so we encourage you to leave reviews and look forward to publishing new and exciting titles each week.

Introduction

Chichén Itzá's Great Ball Court. Photo by Bjørn Christian Tørrissen

Chichén Itzá

Many ancient civilizations have influenced and inspired people in the 21st century, like the Greeks and the Romans, but of all the world's civilizations, none have intrigued people more than the Mayans, whose culture, astronomy, language, and mysterious disappearance all continue to captivate people. At the heart of the fascination is the most visited and the most spectacular of Late Classic Maya cities: Chichén Itzá.

Chichén Itzá was inhabited for hundreds of years and was a very influential center in the later years of Maya civilization. At its height, Chichén Itzá may have had over 30,000 inhabitants, and with a spectacular pyramid, enormous ball court, observatory and several temples, the builders of this city exceeded even those at Uxmal in developing the use of columns and exterior relief decoration. Of particular interest at Chichén Itzá is the sacred cenote, a sinkhole was a focus for Maya rituals around water. Because adequate supplies of water, which rarely collected on the surface of the limestone based Yucatan, were essential for adequate agricultural production, the Maya here considered it of primary importance. Underwater archaeology carried out in the cenote at Chichén Itzá revealed that offerings to the Maya rain deity Chaac (which may have included people) were tossed into the sinkhole.

Although Chichén Itzá was around for hundreds of years, it had a relatively short period of dominance in the region, lasting from about 800-950 CE Today, tourists are taken by guides to a building called the Nunnery for no good reason other than the small rooms reminded the Spaniards of a nunnery back home. Similarly the great pyramid at Chichén Itzá is designated El Castillo ("The Castle"), which it almost certainly was not, while the observatory is called El Caracol ("The Snail") for its spiral staircase. Of course, the actual names for these places were lost as the great Maya cities began to lose their populations, one by one. Chichén Itzá was partially abandoned in 948, and the culture of the Maya survived in a disorganized way until it was revived at Mayapán around 1200. Why Maya cities were abandoned and left to be overgrown by the jungle is a puzzle that intrigues people around the world today, especially those who have a penchant for speculating on lost civilizations.

Mayapán

A panoramic view of Mayapán

Early Mayapán was closely connected to the overshadowing power of the region at the time: the mighty trading city of Chichén Itzá. Mayapán emerged first as a minor settlement in the orbit of Chichén, but it slowly came to replace it after the larger city's trade connections with the Toltecs of Tula crumbled and it suffered a staggering defeat by Mayapán's armies. The building styles and art in their city show both admiring references to the great Chichén Itzá as well as an attempt to position Mayapán as a more orthodox heir of Maya tradition. At the same time, they emulated many features and could not escape the tremendous influences - especially in religion - of Chichén. This is seen in the fact that many of the most important buildings in the new city appear to be small-scale reproductions of ones in Chichén.

Due in part to the fact that it has long been overshadowed by Chichén Itzá, a lot excavation and scholarly research on the site has only come about in recent decades, and even though there is still plenty of work to do, a lot of information about life in Mayapán has been unearthed. At its height, Mayapán may have boasted a population of over 15,000, and archaeologists have had their hands full trying to discover and restore the several thousand buildings both inside Mayapán's walls and outside them as well.

Tikal

Tikal's main plaza during the Winter Solstice. Picture by Bjørn Christian Tørrissen.

The Maya maintained power in the Yucatan for over a thousand years, and at the height of its "Classical era" (3rd-9th centuries CE), the city of Tikal was one of the power centers of the empire. Archaeologists believe Tikal had been built as early as the 5th or 4th century BC, and eventually it became a political, economic and military capital that was an important part of a far-flung network across Mesoamerica, despite the fact it was seemingly conquered by Teotihuacan in the 4th century CE. It seems the foreign rulers came to assimilate Mayan culture, thus ensuring Tikal would continue to be a power base, and as a result, the city would not be abandoned until about the 10th century CE.

As one of the Ancient Maya's most important sites, construction at Tikal was impressive, and even though it was apparently conquered, the city's records were unusually well preserved. This includes a list of the city's dynastic rulers, as well as the tombs and monuments dedicated to them. Thanks to this preservation, Tikal offers researchers their best look at the Ancient Maya and has gone a long way toward helping scholars understand Mayan history.

Uxmal

Palimp Sesto's picture of the ruins of Uxmal

During the Maya's Classical era, the city of Uxmal was one of its most noteworthy places. While it was not as powerful as cities like Tikal, Uxmal was apparently at the forefront of Mayan culture, particularly when it came to architecture. However, while Uxmal used high ground to display its prominence, and the ruins are still among the most popular places for tourists in the region, the site is still shrouded in mystery. Even as scholars continue to work on the site to further interpret it, it's still unclear when exactly Uxmal was founded, how many people called it home, and when it was abandoned, despite the existence of Mayan chronicles and oral legends.

What is apparent, however, is the skills of Uxmal's artisans, whether through constructing structures like the five-level Pyramid of Magicians and the expansive Governor's Palace or adorning the structures with precisely detailed art and sculptures. In fact, the craftsmanship can be credited with helping to preserve Uxmal itself.

The Most Famous Cities of the Maya: The History of Chichén Itzá, Tikal, Mayapán, and Uxmal covers the history of each city, as well as the speculation and debate over the city's buildings. Along with pictures and a bibliography, you will learn about the Mayan cities like never before.

The Most Famous Cities of the Maya: The History of Chichén Itzá, Tikal, Mayapán, and Uxmal

Free Books by Charles River Editors

Discounted Books by Charles River Editors

Tikal

A Note on the Periods of Mayan History

This book follows the traditional system of dividing Mayan history into "periods." Much like European history is divided between the Ancient and Medieval Periods based on whether the Roman Empire had fallen or not, there is a great dividing line in Mayan history called the Classic or Postclassic period.

The apogee of Mayan culture and influence was in the period known to Mesoamerican scholars as the "Classical" period. Ranging from to the 3rd-9th centuries, during this time the region was dominated by two great powers, Tikal and Calakmul, located far to the south of the Yucatán in the northern Highlands. To the west, central Mexico was dominated by the cities of Teotihuacan, Cholula and Monte Albán. This was a period of relative stability, though it probably didn't feel that way as the ruling dynasties of Tikal and Calakmul vied for power and fought numerous proxy wars through their many client states . This period is comparable to the great "cold war" between Athens and Sparta in ancient Greece.

Much like the Roman Empire did not collapse in every area at the same time, the change from the Classic to Postclassic occurred in different places differentially. The Classic Mayan world included a constellation of city-states arranged in great, rival, shifting confederacies. These cities, including the famous centers of Tikal, Palenque, Caracol, and Calakmul, were ruled by kings who were considered semi-divine and were widely commemorated in stone monuments. Eventually, however, the great cities of the Classic Period collapsed, one by one. Far from vanishing, Mayan culture persisted, especially in rural areas, and over time, a new series of cities emerged. While the greatest Classic cities were based in the Highlands of modern Mexico and Guatemala, the Postclassic cities, including Chichén Itzá and Mayapán, emerged in the north in the Yucatan peninsula. Generally speaking, the Postclassic period lasted from the 900s until the arrival of the Spanish in the 1500s.

A Note on Pronunciations and Names

While the Ancient Maya certainly had their own system of writing, the Spanish Conquest ultimately eradicated knowledge of it, so the Mayan languages have been written for almost 500 years using Latin characters adopted from Spanish by missionary priests. Nonetheless, some of the sounds in the Mayan languages do not correspond directly to sounds in English or Spanish, so some guidance is needed for proper pronunciation.

"X" is pronounced as "SH" so the Mayan city of Yaxchilan is pronounced "Ya-sh-i-laan"

"J" is pronounced as a hard "H" so the Mayan name Jasaw is pronounced "Ha-saw"

"Z" is pronounced like an English "S"

"HU" and "UH" are pronounced like a "W" so the Mexican name Teotihuacán is pronounced "Teo-ti-wa-caan"

The Mayan orthography also uses an apostrophe (') to mark a sound that does not appear in most

European languages called a glottal stop. This represents a stoppage of air in the throat, a bit like the swallowing of the "TT" in "LITTLE" when pronounced by a Cockney Englishman (which would be written in Mayan orthography as: "li'le"). The glotttal stop is considered to be a consonant.

While the word "Tikal" is Mayan, it is not the name that the Ancient Maya gave to the city when they lived in it. The modern name comes from the Mayan "Ti' ak'al" or "At the Waterhole," a name given by Mayan hunters who traveled through the area and stopped at water reservoirs in the ancient city. The exact name has been lost, but it appears that it was written using a glyph that represented a topknot hair style. Hence, it was probably given the same name, "Mutal." In more formal occasions, it was likely called "Yax Mutal" ("First Topknot"). As a result, some modern archaeologists use the name "Mutal" for talking about the city, but to avoid confusion, this book will stick with the more common name Tikal throughout.[1]

The emblem glyph representing the name Mutal.

As scholars have increasingly learned to read the sophisticated writing system left behind by the Maya, they have gained a more subtle understanding of their naming practices. Generally speaking, only the names of kings and queens, as well as a few other individuals, are named in the records, and early archaeologists used names that described the name glyphs, with names like "Stormy Sky," "Curl Snout" or "Great Jaguar Paw." Today it's possible to reconstruct the actual sounds of names like Siyaj Chan K'awiil II , Yax Nuun Ayiin I, or Chak Tok Ich'aak I, but these names are quite long and contain many repetitive elements (much like the continual repetition of the names George and Edward among English kings). This can quickly get confusing for readers, so when this book refers to a king, the Mayan pronunciation will come first, followed by the English glyph names. Subsequent references to the kings will then use the English glyph names to help readers follow along. That said, there are a few

---

1 *Chronicle of the Maya Kings and Queens: Deciphering the Dynasties of the Ancient Maya* by Simon Martin and Nikolai Grube (2000). Thames and Hudson, London. Pg 30

exceptions to this due to the growing prominence of the Mayan names for these individuals, most importantly the great king Jasaw Chan K'awiil I.

A jade statue depicting Jasaw Chan K'awiil I

The names of the early kings after Yax Ehb' Xook are largely unimportant to history because of a lack of definitive information about their lives and deeds. One exception is from 317 AD, when there was a break in the male line and the city was ruled by its first recorded woman: queen Lady Une' B'alam ("Baby Jaguar"). This set an important precedent for later claims of succession in the city when usurpers of various shades would look to their own matrilineal ancestors as justification for their place on the throne[2].

---

2   Martin and Grube (2000), Pg 27

Chapter 1: Early Tikal

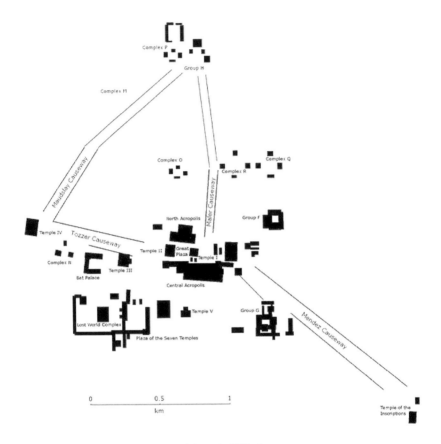

A layout of Tikal

Given how old the city of Tikal is, it's no surprise that the actual origins of the city and the date of its first settlement have been lost to time. In fact, the city was so old that it seems to have predated the Maya's invention of writing, and it was not recorded by later generations, likely because they were more concerned with the founding of the First Dynasty. Thus, the only information historians can glean regarding dates comes from archaeological excavations at the tomb-temple complex of the North Acropolis. The North Acropolis is not only ancient but was sacred and central to the political, religious and social lives of communities for centuries, similar to Westminster Abbey or the Acropolis in Ancient Athens. The Ancient Mayans who lived in Tikal and were unaware of the city's origins itself viewed the North Acropolis not only as ancient but as a symbol of their national identity and sense of self. Thus far, archaeologists have determined that the oldest date for a building at the North Acropolis is about 350 BC, though traces of settlement likely went back centuries before that.[3] By the time the city fell over a millennium later, it had become a complex jumble of construction, a "labyrinth of elevated platforms and walls.[4]"

3   Martin and Grube (2000), Pgs 26 and 43
4   *Exploring Mesoamerica: Places in Time* by John M.D. Pohl (1999). Oxford University Press, NY. Pg 70

Pictures of the ruins of the North Acropolis

The city of Tikal was founded in a favorable position along the southern edge of a north-south mountain range that divides the Peten region. Around Tikal, settlers enjoyed a number of varied environments. From the swampy bottomlands called "bajos", they collected crocodiles, frogs, water lilies and logwood trees. Along the hills, they raised corn and other crops and navigated the river valleys as trade routes, bringing up useful items like shells, seaweed and stingray spines from the coast of what is today Belize[5]. The city that they founded would eventually become the longest-inhabited Classical center, with an estimated 39 recorded rulers.

It appears that the early inhabitants of Tikal worshiped "spirit forces personified by [a] giant birdlike stucco mask.[6]" These masks have been found in the temples of the North Acropolis, and archaeologists have uncovered similar monuments in other contemporary Lowland Pre-Classic cities like El Mirador, Nakbé, Cerros and Uaxactun. There is no consensus on exactly what god or goddess was represented by the masks, but there are two potential candidates based on documents that survived the Spanish and records kept by the Spanish themselves. In the Highland mythological text *Popoh Vuh*, there is one candidate called "Vucub Caquix," a lord of twilight who dominated the earth before he was displaced

---

5   *The Lords of Tikal: Rulers of An Ancient Maya City* by Peter D. Harrison (1999) by Thames and Hudson, London. Pgs 45-47.

6   Pohl (1999) pg 70

by the hero twins Hunahpu and Xbalanque. Another possibility is the creator god Itzamna, who was recorded as being revered by the Maya of the Yucatec peninsula by the Franciscan priest Diego de Landa. The interpretation of the North Acropolis monuments and the surrounding temples varies greatly depending on whether this figure is a dark lord of the era before humans or a beloved creator. Of course, it is also possible that this deity, who was worshiped in a period of great antiquity, was displaced by the emergence of later gods like Tlaloc or Quetzalcoatl. Regardless, there are no known written accounts of this deity's name.

Once it emerged as a political unit worthy of mention, early Tikal was dominated by two sister-cities located roughly 20 miles (32 km) to the northwest. These were El Mirador and Nakbé, cities which adopted an elaborate Mesoamerican urban tradition from groups like the Olmecs further north. This included stone buildings, temples on top of pyramids, the ball game,[7] and the construction of stone monuments. The most important of these monuments to emerge out of the El Mirador/Nakbé tradition were "stelae" (the plural of "stela"), which were large stone slabs covered in elaborate carvings commemorating important events. Similar to royal inscriptions in ancient Egypt, kings in Tikal would erect these stelae to commemorate great victories, important calendric events (the equivalent of decades and centenaries), investitures of power, and deaths. Since little of the early Mayan writing has survived the ravages of time and the Spanish Conquest, these stelae are often important sources of information about what the kings wanted observers to know about themselves[8].

---

7   A sport that combined game with ritual, involving stone courts and players who attempted to knock rubber balls through stone hoops without the use of their hands.
8   Pohl (1999) pgs 68-70

Picture of a stela in Tikal

The ballgame court at Tikal. Picture by Simon Burchell.

Chapter 2: The First Dynasty

By 300 AD, the El Mirador/Nakbé political entity was crumbling, so its various vassal states were able to act independently, including not only Tikal but other major players of later history like Uaxactun and Calakmul. In this vacuum of power emerged what anthropologists call "chiefdoms," relatively simple units ruled by a single leader (the chief) and his personal bodyguard who is able to extract tribute from surrounding farmers. Chiefs might in turn send tribute up the line to a larger, paramount chief who controlled a number of lesser chiefdoms[9].

It was out of this relatively chaotic and occasionally brutal situation that Tikal's leadership began to consolidate local power, and eventually the rulers established a system to transfer power from one generation to the next. They also created basic bureaucratic institutions, such as a priesthood, which gave further continuity and regularity to government. During this process, they undoubtedly looked to the examples of El Mirador and Nakbé, as well as other neighboring cities. In time, what emerged was the creation of the First Dynasty.

The early information about the First Dynasty is largely unavailable because much of it was destroyed via the elimination of the city's early monuments in 378 AD, but even if they had survived, the records would have been spotty because of the lack of sophistication in Mayan writing at the time.

9   Pohl (1999) pgs 67-68

It would be some time before the people of Tikal themselves were involved in perfecting writing; in fact, contemporary records were only kept starting around 292 AD, so everything that scholars can piece together about the earlier eras of the First Dynasty have come from what was written by subsequent generations of Tikal's residents after the fact.[10]

As a result, scholars' estimates of the dates of the reigns of the early monarchs are based upon a technique called average reign length estimates. Simon Martin, a historian of the region, compiled all of the known start and end dates for the reigns of Mayan kings and queens and created an average of 22.5 years. He was then able to put them onto undated lists of kings, such as those available for early Tikal[11]. While this system obviously does not always (or even most of the time) provide the correct date, it offers up the best technique for dating events like the founding of the First Dynasty.

At the same time, knowledge of those early days has improved over the last few decades as historians unearth new information about the First Dynasty. For example, scholars long thought that Great Jaguar Paw, the last ruler of the dynasty, was the 9th in his line, but recent findings have uncovered the names of four more early kings. When added to the average reign length technique, this pushes back the reign of Yax Ehb' Xook (First Step Shark) to roughly 90 AD and opens up the possibility that his remains are those found in a splendid, sumptuous tomb called Burial 85 at the North Acropolis[12].

What is clear is that royal life in early Tikal centered around the Great Plaza, a broad paved area between the North Acropolis temple-tombs and the Central Acropolis, a complex structure that included administrative facilities, courts of law, and administrative areas. It was in splendor here that the First Dynasty constructed their empire. Other elite families tended to have their own homes scattered around the neighboring hills and farms, where they could control the local population[13].

---

10 Martin and Grube (2000), Pg 26
11 "The Painted King List: A Commentary on Codex-Style Dynastic Vases." by Simon Martin in *The Maya Vase Book: A Corpus of Rollout Photographs of Maya Vases by Justin Kerr, Volume 5*, edited by Barbara Kerr and Justin Kerr, pp. 847-867. Kerr Associates, New York.
12 Martin and Grube (2000), Pgs 26-27
13 Harrison (1999) pgs 73-75

Royal residences in Tikal. Picture by Dennis Jarvis.

Temple I with the North Acropolis to the left and Center Acropolis to the right.

One definitive element of the political life of the First Dynasty was the city's conflict with its primary political rival, the nearby city of Uaxactun. In many ways, Uaxactun remains in the record as a ghostly twin, mostly because its eventual conquest by Tikal meant that its early history was erased and that it remained in Tikal's shadow after that. However, it seems that early Uaxactun was nearly equal in power, making the two legitimate rivals. Like Tikal, Uaxactun emerged out of the chaos of the collapse of the old Nakbé and El Mirador power structure, but the eventual conquest of Uaxactun by the Second Dynasty after the Teotihuacano Entrada would solidify the city of Tikal as the dominant power in the region[14].

The last king of the First Dynasty was one of the most important. Chak Tok Ich'aak I, whose name is written as either Great Burning Paw or (more commonly) Great Jaguar Paw, came to the throne around roughly 360 AD, and it was during his reign that the city began to look outward in a much greater way than before. Much of this outward looking perspective involved the importation of goods and ideas from Central Mexico, specifically Teotihuacán; trade had existed for some time, but it reached new levels of sophistication during this period, especially involving high quality ceramics. As discussed further below, Great Jaguar Paw may have written his own death warrant, because it seems that the Teotihuacano army traveled along these same trade routes to come kill him. Another direct impact of this contact was the creation of the Lost World Complex[15].

---

14 Pohl (1999) pg 72

Perhaps the most important construction during the rule of the First Dynasty was a complex of temples and support buildings poetically called the Mundo Perdido (or "Lost World"). Located at the western edge of the city center, it was the largest temple complex in the Preclassical city, dominated by a large four-sided pyramid topped with three temples, some of which may have been used as solar observatories to chart solstices and equinoxes. The architectural impact of the Mexican contact on the Lost World complex can be seen as early as 250 AD, long before Great Jaguar Paw's trade contacts[16].

One of the more important elements of the Lost World's architectural style is that it was the first area of Tikal to utilize a style called "Talud-Tablero." Unlike an Egyptian pyramid with four smooth sides, Mesoamerican pyramids were built like layer cakes or steps, with ever-smaller square blocks placed on top of one another. The Talud-Tablero style, also called the "slop and panel" style, is characterized by "pairs of taludes [sloped layers] and framed tableros [horizontal layers] that pass completely around a platform , and stairs flanked by balustrades that are capped with finial blocks (called *remates*)."[17] This is important because the style originated not amongst the Maya but in the mighty Central Mexican city of Teotihuacán. The interaction between Tikal and this distant imperial capital would come to dominate Tikal's political fortunes in the coming years, but the Lost World also shows the importance of Mexican styles at an early date in Tikal.

15 Martin and Grube (2000), pg 28
16 *Ibid*
17 "Architectural Aspects of Interaction between Tikal and Teotihuacan" by Juan Pedro Laporte in *The Maya and Teotihuacan: Reinterpreting Early Classic Interaction* (2003) by Geoffrey E. Braswell (ed.). University of Austin Press. pg 200

One of the Lost World pyramids. Picture by Dennis Jarvis.

A Lost World Temple. Picture by Mike Murga.

The roof of Temple III.

A step pyramid that's part of "Complex Q" in Tikal.

Chapter 3: The Entrada, Teotihuacán, and the Second Dynasty

The destiny of Tikal was forever changed on January 31st, 378 AD when a massive army arrived at the city's gates. This event has become known by the Spanish name "Entrada" which means simply the "Entry," as in "the entry of Teotihuacán". While there is no clear record of the events due to the sheer scale of destruction that took place, it's clear neither Tikal nor the Maya as a whole had ever seen anything like it because these foreign soldiers not only conquered but also subsequently ruled Tikal despite the fact they had come from Teotihuacán in Central Mexico, about 630 miles (1013 kilometers) away.[18] In short order, the Teotihuacanos dispatched the rulers of Tikal and installed their own people to rule, which ironically resulted in positioning Tikal as the largest and most important city in the Mayan lands. In the process, the Teotihuacanos not only changed Tikal but the direction of the Mayan civilization for centuries to come.

This conquest came about after trade contacts were established between the Mayan regions and what is today Central Mexico. These contacts went back centuries and included the transfer of not only goods but also ideas. An early example of this was the Talud-Tablero architecture found in the Lost World Complex of Tikal, and another clearly identifiable Mexican import found in early Tikal is green-

---

18 Martin and Grube (2000), Pgs 29

hued obsidian, which can be clearly identified to sites in Mexico[19].

Early contacts between the Teotihuacanos and the Maya of Tikal and other cities began in the western Mayan city of Kaminaljuyu, which became wealthy acting as a go-between for the two peoples[20]. Tikal's trade was primarily with the city of Teotihuacán, which was located in the Valley of Mexico near today's Mexico City. Thriving between 100-750 AD, this was one of the largest cities in the ancient world, with a population of at least 200,000. In comparison, when Tikal was at the height of its power in the 8th century, it had a population of around 60,000. Teotihuacán was a supremely well-planned and efficient city that was able to field massive armies and extend its power far beyond its home base to create a unified empire of the type that was never possible in the less fertile Mayan lands[21].

The ruins of Teotihuacán

There is a long-standing debate over exactly how much influence Teotihuacán (and Central Mexico in general) had over the development of the Mayan heartland. Mayanists have long been protective of their region and have tended to downplay Mexican influence and emphasize Mayan creativity. Before the decipherment of the Mayan script, they argued that Mayan leaders emulated styles from Teotihuacán but had no direct contact or rule[22]. In this interpretation, what happened in 378 was that

19 *Ibid*
20 "Understanding Early Classic Interaction Between Kaminaljuyu and Central Mexico" by Geoffrey E. Braswell in *The Maya and Teotihuacan: Reinterpreting Early Classic Interaction* (2003) by Geoffrey E. Braswell (ed.). University of Austin Press. pgs 105-142
21 Pohl (1999) pgs 53-66
22 "Forward" in *The Maya and Teotihuacan: Reinterpreting Early Classic Interaction* (2003) by Geoffrey E. Braswell

Great Jaguar Paw, who had initiated trade with Teotihuacán, died and was replaced by his son, Lord Curl Snout, who formalized the trade relationship and began a period of stylistic emulation of their trade partners[23]. However, over time, archaeologists and historians have found evidence that the transfer of power in 378 from Great Jaguar Paw to Curl Snout - while it may have been inspired by earlier trade contacts - was anything but peaceful.

Today, there is a general consensus that Tikal was conquered by a mighty army, and the rumors of the conquering army's march must have preceded it, as such a force could not move quickly without horses (which arrived with the Europeans). The first record historians have of its movements comes from a smaller city called El Perú, roughly 49 miles (78 kilometers) to the west of Tikal. El Perú fell on January 23rd, and the armies arrived at Tikal eight days later after traveling up the San Pedro Martir River.[24]

At the head of this army was a figure called Siyaj K'ak' ("Fire Born"), who appears to have been a general. The surviving writing says that Siyaj K'ak' was sent at the head of the army at the behest of a mysterious figure called "Spearthrower Owl." This name is not written out using Mayan script but is instead an image of an owl bearing an atlatl (a device for throwing spears). The owl may have been a symbol of a warrior god or caste in the city, but the name "Spearthrower Owl" appears more likely to be a title than the actual name of the person. Traditionally, Spearthrower Owl has been thought of as the ruler of Teotihuacán who sponsored the expedition, based on some monuments that appear to place the date of his ascension to a throne (which throne is not certain, but it's not Tikal's) on May 4th, 374 and his death on June 10th, 439. The records also suggest he took a Mayan wife[25]. However, recently there has been a debate over whether the title actually refers to a god, because some murals found at Teotihuacán refer to a site called "Spearthrower Owl Hill", and these murals are roughly contemporaneous with the Entrada of 378. In this understanding, Spearthrower Owl is a martial god similar to the later Aztec god Huitzilopochtli. The archaeologists and historians will have to find further evidence (including a search for Spearthrower Owl Hill) before a more definitive statement on the subject can be made.[26]

Either way, when this army arrived, the Maya likely resisted, but Tikal had no walls, a defensive feature that would not appear in Mayan cities until centuries later. It also seems that the resistance didn't do much harm to the armies of Teotihuacán, which quickly conquered other cities as well. Images found on pottery depict the arrival of the Mexican warriors and ambassadors and the death of Great Jaguar Paw on January 31st, 378. More direct evidence of conquest comes from Uaxactun, where a mural image depicts a submissive Maya and a dominant Teotihuacano from the time period[27]. It is useful to compare this image to the type of imagery found at the city of Chichén Itzá some 600 years later. There is a similar debate at Chichén about a possible invasion by a Central Mexican power (this time the Toltec Empire), but there is no record there of conquest and no images of Mayans

(ed.). University of Austin Press. pgs xiii-xvi
23 Pohl (1999) pg 72
24 Martin and Grube (2000), Pg 29
25 Martin and Grube (2000), Pg 30
26 "Spearthrower Owl Hill: A Toponym at Atatelco, Teotihuacan" by Jesper Nielsen and Christopher Helmke (2008) in the journal *Latin American Antiquity* 19(4), pgs. 459-474.
27 *Ibid*

dominated by Mexicans[28].

There is also archaeological evidence for a change in the nature of the Mexican-Mayan contact at this point as well. For example, Tikal became home to considerably more Teotihuacano objects after 378, especially lidded tripods coated in painted stucco. Even more notable is the fact that there was a systematic destruction of monuments from before 378, and the use of the broken stone as either fill for new construction projects or their exportation to other, less important cities. For a royal system whose legitimacy was founded upon a connection to the past (especially in the form of the tombs of the North Acropolis), the destruction of these past records indicate a major political break occurred on that year[29].

A stucco mask adorning a temple in the North Acropolis. Picture by Bjørn Christian Tørrissen.

It's also known that during the same year, an army out of Tikal finally conquered Uaxactun and eliminated its ruling line. In its place, the brother of the lord of Tikal, a man named Lord Smoking Frog, was put on the throne and founded his own cadet dynasty that would rule in the shadow of Tikal[30].

The last date scholars have for the fall of a surrounding city was 381. The Teotihuacanos would put up their own dynasties at all of these sites, but it's unclear what the relationship between Tikal and

---

28 A copy of the image can be found on the Website of the Museo Popol Vuh of the Universidad Francisco Marroquin, accessed online at: http://www.popolvuh.ufm.edu/exhibiciones/u-wach-ulew/uwach05.htm
29 Martin and Grube (2000), Pg 30
30 Pohl (1999) pg 71

these other conquests was, or if there was an effective central coordination. If there was, it would eventually break down in the wars that would emerge a few generations later[31].

Regardless of whether Spearthrower Owl was a man or a god, he was not the titular ruler of Tikal for long, because the record suggests that his son, Yax Nuun Ayiin I ("Curl Snout") took the throne on September 12, 379. This date marks the beginning of the Second Dynasty, and Curl Snout would reign for 25 years until his death on June 17, 404. When he came to the throne, Curl Snout was only a boy, and it appears that the general Siyaj held the reins of power as a regent over the city during Curl Snout's youth.

A stela at Tikal that depicts Curl Snout. Picture by H. Grobe.

While Curl Snout would not live to a ripe old age (if Spearthrower Owl was a man, he apparently outlived his son by 35 years), his reign was notable as the high watermark of Teotihucano imperialism

---

31 Martin and Grube (2000), Pg 39

in the region. This was when the monuments dating before 378 were destroyed, and the regime aimed to re-create the royal imagery of Central Mexico in its monuments and murals. This first generation of conquerors had no connections to the land they ruled and derived their legitimacy from their distant patron Spearthrower Owl, but Curl Snout did marry a wife with Mayan royal titles, so there was at least a nominal attempt to associate the Second Dynasty with the previous power structure.[32] It is believed that Curl Snout was buried in the magnificent Burial 10 in Temple 34, which was the first building to break out of the traditional front face of the North Acropolis (though others would follow in later generations)[33].

Upon Curl Snout's death, his heir was not yet considered an adult, so just as Siyaj K'ak' ruled as a regent during Curl Snout's youth, another non-royal by the name of Siyaj Chan K'inich ("Sky Born Sun God") would rule from 406-411. After sitting under the thumb of the regent Siyaj Chan K'inich for five years, the new king, Siyaj Chan K'awiil II (Lord Stormy Sky), ascended to the throne of Tikal on November 26, 411. He would have a particularly long and productive reign before he died on February 3, 456 (45 years, twice the average).

32 Martin and Grube (2000), Pgs 32-33
33 *Ibid*

A stela depicting Stormy Sky

The reign of Lord Stormy Sky was characterized by a re-emergence of Mayan imagery in royal propaganda and an emphasis on the continuity of the Second Dynasty with the royalty of the First Dynasty through his mother's line. This was a distinct break with the imagery of his father's reign, which depicted the Maya only as subservient and was dominated by imported Mexican symbols. In fact, there was a conscious use of archaisms in the art; for instance, artisans basically re-created a 150 year old stela with only slightly different wording. The words of other monuments also placed an emphasis on the precedence of royal blood being transferred via the female line in the case of the 4th century queen, Lady Une' B'alam[34]. Furthermore, emphasis was taken off of ritual at the consciously Mexican Lost World complex and returned to the thoroughly Mayan North Acropolis. Other evidence of the change is that the royal regalia depicted in the stelae returned to the traditional Maya form

---

34 Martin and Grube (2000), Pg 34; Mesoamerica 72

created in the 3rd century, and this would remain basically unchanged until the collapse of the city. Even the king's name - possibly a regnal name[35] - was a reference to an earlier king, Stormy Sky, who ascended to the throne around 307 AD[36].

What inspired the triumphant Teotihuacanos to "nativize" and emphasize the Mayan culture and dynastic tradition that they had previously scorned? The written and archaeological records are mostly silent on this, but it's possible to make comparisons to similar cases around the world where an invading warrior elite conquers a wide swath of territory. Examples would include the French Normans in Britain, the Hellenic Greeks in much of their post-Alexander empire, the Turkic Safavid Dynasty in Persia, and the Manchus in China. In all of these cases, the elite established not only a dominant dynasty but also installed smaller lines throughout the new territory, and in the process, they spread themselves quite thin. The conquering Teotihuacanos must have needed to learn to speak the local language to communicate not only with the peasantry but with Tikal's local administrators and bureaucrats, and over time, subsequent generations of the elite who grew up communicating with the locals likely had no direct experience or emotional ties to their native homeland. Moreover, they may have resented having to send tribute back "home" and may have further assimilated in efforts to legitimize themselves to avoid local uprisings.

One long-term effect of this period of strength, during which Tikal-Teotihuacán influence spread throughout the Mayan Lowlands, was a reinforcement of the dynastic system. In fact, while Tikal had been an early pioneer in this form of governance, it was only with the influence of Teotihuacán's Mexican tradition that it reached its peak. Tikal's dominance also helped spread the cult of the rain god Tlaloc (who became known by the Mayan name Chaak) throughout the Mayan lands, where he displaced the earlier bird-faced deity as the principal god[37]. There has been some argument that this dynastic and religious tradition fostered opposition amongst more conservative Mayan groups and helped garner support for Tikal's enemies in traditionalist Calakmul, which claimed royal descent from El Mirador.

---

35 A name chosen by a king or other ruler at the time of his or her ascension. A modern example would be the names of popes, so Jorge Mario Bergoglio became Pope Francis I.
36 "Tikal's Dynastic Rulers" accessed online at: http://www.tikalpark.com/dynasty.htm
37 Martin and Grube (2000), Pg 35

A Classical era depiction of Chaak

Chapter 4: The Great Hiatus and the Third Dynasty

As archaeologists began to piece together Tikal's history in the mid-20th century, they encountered a confusing problem. Between 562 and 692 - a full 130 years - not a single dated monument was built in the city, nor were there any large construction projects. It was as if the leadership of the city had simply left for over a century. Further complicating this picture is the fact that many Early Classic monuments that predate 550 AD were vandalized[38]. This time became known as the "Hiatus", but today, scholars have a much richer understanding of this period. The lack of monuments at Tikal during the Hiatus no longer hinders an understanding of the period as much as it previously did because much has been learned from decorated commemorative ceramics and monuments in other cities.

Far from being a period of quiescence, it is now known that this period was marked by chaos, political intrigue, and war. The roots of the Hiatus begin in a troubled period between 508 and 562. After the death of Chak Tok Ich'aak on July 24, 508, there appears to have been a vacuum of power, which was made perfectly clear 13 days later when the relatively weak city of Yaxchilan captured one of Tikal's vassal cities. The exact events after this are largely lost because most of the stelae are defaced or unfinished, but it appears that Tikal's elite became divided between two factions.

Around this time, a figure called the "Lady of Tikal" appeared on the stage. A daughter of Chak Tok Ich'aak, she was only four years old when her father died and was undoubtedly a pawn of a larger faction, at least initially. She appears on stelae in 511, 514, and 527, but always in association with a

---

38 Pohl (1999) pg 74

male co-ruler, and in 527, she was depicted as ruling alongside Kaloomte' B'alam, a general involved in the 486 attack on the city of Maasal and usually considered the 19th king of Tikal. However, somewhere between 527 and 537, she becomes associated with the 20th king, lord "Bird Claw."

By 557, fortunes appear to have shifted, as another king, "Double Bird", is marked as the 21st king. Double Bird was also the child of Chak Tok Ich'aak II, born in January 508, only seven months before his father's death. He is commemorated as having come to power on January 29, 537, and the monuments record him as having "returned" (presumably from exile) during this period.[39]

As these records suggest, the death of Chak Tok Ich'aak II led to dynastic strife, with different elements of his court seizing his two young children as pawns to make separate claims to the throne. Meanwhile, the internal divisions of the city meant that Tikal' elites were unable to maintain their control on wider Mayan politics. In 553, Double Bird is recorded as sponsoring the ruler in distant Caracol, but in the same year, the far closer kingdom of Naranjo became a vassal of the rival city of Calakmul. This was followed in 556 by a direct war with the now-rebellious Caracol, where Tikal lost a vassal to the upstart city. Finally, in 562 there was an event called a "star war", a war that was timed to coincide with the movements of Venus. During this war, an army likely consisting of the combined forces of Caracol and Calakmul overran Tikal and ritually killed Double Bird.

It's certainly noteworthy that early archaeological studies have documented the simultaneous collapses of Teotihuacán and Tikal, but it's unclear how or whether the two are linked. Did Teotihuacán recall its soldiers from Tikal? Was the fall of Teotihuacán seen as a withdrawal of divine mandate and something that might have galvanized Tikal's enemies? Another theory is that the collapse was brought about by the collapse of trade and the inability of Tikal's elites to maintain their own trade routes. Regardless of exactly what the connections were between the collapse of Tikal and Teotihuacán, 562 AD was a momentous one in Mesoamerica because it witnessed the collapse of the region's mightiest city and the conquest and subjugation of its second-most powerful.

Debates over the internal divisions in Tikal and the effects of the collapse of Teotihuacán also overshadow the fact that the collapse of Tikal's hegemony was at least partly a product of a geopolitical strategy by two rivals: Caracol and, especially, Calakmul. Calakmul was, like Tikal, an inheritor of the ancient Preclassic era, having emerged from being a vassal of El Mirador and Nakbé. The capital of the kingdom was located 24 miles (39 km) to the north of the ruins of old El Mirador and seemed to have claimed to be the rightful heir of that ancient city. In this way, the rulers of Calakmul leapfrogged over Tikal and Teotihuacán, effectively asserting themselves as the true heirs of the Mayan civilization.

Calakmul and the kingdom it ruled, called Kaan (the Kingdom of the Snake), remained in the shadow of Tikal during Tikal's glory days, but the kingdom was never conquered by Tikal or the Teotihuacanos. In the 540s, Calakmul began to cement power and began implementing a strategy to displace Tikal. King Stone Hand Jaguar and then King Sky Witness worked throughout the 540s and 550s to bring to heel one small city after another in order to create a ring of enemies around Tikal. In the process, they apparently hoped to be able to starve Tikal politically by denying it tribute from vassals and preventing it from reconstituting trade networks to Central Mexico that were in decline

---

39 Martin and Grube (2000), Pg 39

with the collapse of Teotihuacán.

It appears that despite their divisions, the Tikal elites were aware of this strategy, at least after Sky Witness' troops brought Caracol under his banner in 561[40]. Tikal's last Second Dynasty king, Lord Double Bird, ordered an attack on Caracol in 562, no doubt hoping to break the stranglehold that Calakmul had created. Unfortunately, he underestimated the strength of his enemies or perhaps overestimated his own power. He not only failed to take Caracol in that attack but subsequently lost everything in the alliance's counterattack[41].

Sometime around 593 AD, a new king is recorded as ascending to the throne of Tikal: King Animal Skull, 22nd in the line. There is evidence to show that this ascension involved the rise of a third dynasty to power. For one, there is an oblique reference to the ritual killing of Double Bird, and the pottery made for Animal Skull makes much of his matrilineal connections to Tikal's elite but is completely silent about his father. In fact, scholars' understanding of the line of the earliest kings comes from retrospective ceramics that trace his lineage. Both of these elements give weight to the argument that Animal Skull was part of a new ruling family put into power by the victorious Caracol and Calakmul, a common occurrence in Mayan conquests[42].

In the normal course of events, this conquest should have been the political end of Tikal. A typical example would be Tikal's old rival Uaxactun, which became a minor player after its conquest. There's no doubt that the victorious powers of Caracol and Calakmul had much at stake in keeping Tikal under their thumb.

After the death of Animal Skull in 628 AD, there appears to have been a relatively orderly transition, as his tomb was constructed immediately and was well made and adorned. However, this unity was not to last, as a schism appears to have occurred as early as 648 AD. Roughly 70 miles (112 kilometers) to the southwest of Tikal, a new city named Dos Pilas had a king, B'alaj Chan K'awiil, who claimed to be the legitimate ruler of Tikal. His ascension to the throne was backed by Calakmul[43], but meanwhile, back in Tikal, a ruler named Nuun Ujol Chaak ("Shield Skull") - a rival of B'alaj Chan K'awiil in Dos Pilas - took the throne.

In response, Yuknoom the Great of Calakmul launched another star war in 657 to eject the upstart, but the results of this conflict are confusing. Shield Skull fled Tikal to the distant city of Palenque (another enemy of Calakmul), but B'alaj Chan K'awiil and the Dos Pilas elites seemingly did not return in triumph to Tikal. It's unclear why this happened, but some have speculated that Calakmul decided to rule the city directly. Shield Skull is recorded as being present in Palenque in 659, but he eventually retook Tikal and then Dos Pilas itself in 672. Yet again, Calakmul attacked Shield Skull's forces and drove him out of Dos Pilas in 677, and he was defeated once and for all in 679 AD[44]. While scholars aren't certain, it seems that the Third Dynasty continued in exile in Dos Pilas until around 807 AD.

---

40 Martin and Grube (2000), Pg 104
41 Pohl (1999) pg 74
42 Martin and Grube (2000), Pg 40-42
43 Martin and Grube (2000), Pg 42
44 Martin and Grube (2000), Pgs 42, 57

To understand Tikal during the Hiatus, one helpful comparison is 20th century China. Internally divided and beset by enemies, the traditional dynasty (the Second Dynasty in Tikal or the Manchus in China) was overthrown and puppet rulers - perhaps with ideological ties to foreign powers - are put into place (Tikal's Third Dynasty and the pro-Western government of Chiang Kai Shek), and the nation is ringed with enemy states (Naranjo, Caracol and others for Tikal and Japan, Korea and India for China). When revolution topples the government, a rump of survivors flees and establishes a petty domain under the protection of the former masters, for whom it is useful to recognize the exiles as the legitimate government (in these cases, Dos Pilas and Taiwan).

Despite his overall failure to restore Tikal to glory, Shield Skull was successful in igniting the embers of his city's independence and power, something his son was to see through. This son, Jasaw Chan K'awiil I, was possibly the most important ruler in the long history of Tikal.

An altar depicting Jasaw Chan K'awiil I

Chapter 5: Jasaw Chan K'awiil I and the Fourth Dynasty

The most famous building at Tikal, and arguably one of the most famous and evocative buildings in all of the Mayan kingdoms, is the plainly named Temple I. Temple I, which stands 154 feet (47 meters), is not the tallest building at the site, but its incredibly steep sides, crowning temple, and the existence of its mirror in Temple II across the plaza all give it a remarkable quality that visitors have noted for centuries. The tomb sits hard against the North Acropolis, but it is not properly part of that complex; in essence, Temples I and II dramatically frame the Acropolis. It is perhaps fitting that the tomb of Jasaw Chan K'awiil I - the greatest king of Tikal – both gives a nod to the burial traditions of the North Acropolis but also breaks them, because after Jasaw, no other king would be buried in the ancient halls of their ancestors.

The back of Temple I

The front of Temple I. Picture by Dennis Jarvis.

Jasaw Chan K'awiil faced an uphill battle when he came to power on May 3, 682. He viewed himself as a restorer of Tikal, but he probably had little to work with: his father's armies had been defeated five years earlier, a rival dynasty claimed his throne in Dos Pilas, and it is possible that enemies occupied his capital city. While he may have had some help from his father's allies in Palenque, the fact that he overcame all of these challenges and finally defeated the armies of Calakmul in open battle on August 5, 695 is a testament to his skill as an administrator, diplomat and tactician[45].

As a restorer, Jasaw Chan K'awiil sought to remind his city of its former glories, so he openly revived the symbolism of long-fallen Teotihuacán, especially its regalia (much in the same way that Europeans would use Roman symbolism centuries after that empire's collapse). He had an eye for the past, including hosting the commemoration of his 695 battle on September 14 in order to also commemorate

---

45 Martin and Grube (2000), Pg 44

the 13th K'atun anniversary (256 years - an auspicious number) of the death of his Teotihuacano progenitor Spearthrower Owl[46].

After breaking the stranglehold of Calakmul's noose around Tikal, Jasaw Chan K'awiil began to recreate the old empire. He may have taken Masaal and Naranjo as the spoils of the 695 victory (though he had to put down rebellions in Naranjo later), and he must have taken great satisfaction in sacking Dos Pilas in 705. By 711, he had retaken the cities of Motul de San José, El Perú and Uaxactun. Once these conquests were complete and the Noose was broken, Jasaw Chan K'awiil set about a large number of building projects in the capital before his death in 731 AD.

Despite his emphasis on continuity with the ancient past and his obvious assertions of the inheritance of Teotihuacán's legitimacy, Jasaw Chan K'awiil appears to have been the founder of the Fourth (and final) Dynasty at Tikal. Of course, historians don't know (and probably never will) whether Jasaw Chan K'awiil was actually the direct inheritor of Double Bird, the last Second Dynasty ruler, but either way, he was succeeded by several generations of rulers. His son Yik'in Chan K'awiil, the 27th king, ascended in 734 and built upon his father's triumphs to strengthen the empire, forever shattering Calakmul's desire to dominate in a series of military campaigns that also reshaped the center of Tikal and reflected its return to grandeur.

At the city's height around this time, it had over 60,000 inhabitants covering 10 square miles (25 square kilometers)[47]. This period of strength continued through two more kings until the reign of Yax Nuun Ayiin II in 794 AD. During the city's peak, its merchants were trading in, salt, cotton, cacao, obsidian, jade, and feathers, and the city dominated the region's rivers and ports, reconstituting trade networks that had declined during the Hiatus.[48]

Chapter 6: The Collapse

At the start of the 9th century, it may have seemed to Tikal's residents that the city had passed its darkest days and would rule the region for another six centuries, but in reality, the city and its sociopolitical order would soon be history. This period would become famously known as the Mayan Collapse.

After the relative prosperity of Yax Nuun Ayiin, the Tikal elites once again went quiet. The important ritual date of the 10th Bak'tun in 830 was not commemorated in stone, one part of a 60 year period known as the Second Hiatus during which there were no monuments. Between the years of 809 and 869, there is no evidence of any central authority in the city; while there must have been some form of order, there is nothing to suggest that it was a traditional dynasty with pretensions to the classic power.

In 869, Jasaw Chan K'awiil II, a name likely chosen in homage to the famous king of the past, had a stela erected in his honor as king of Tikal, but he was unable to prevent rulers in Tikal's small vassal cities from asserting their claims to Tikal's throne, something that had never occurred before. The last

46 Martin and Grube (2000), Pg 45
47 Pohl (1999) pg 68
48 Pohl (1999) pg 73

monument built in the city was in 889 AD, and while the city was not immediately abandoned (there is archaeological evidence of settlements there lasting until the late 10th or early 11th centuries), the subsequent generations of residents did not even maintain the pretence of dynastic rule. In fact, some of the residents actually squatted in the palaces and temples and mined the North Acropolis tombs for their treasures. Similarly, in Dos Pilas, crude earthworks were built that cut right across old roads, courtyards and even buildings[49]. There is also evidence that local groups in the region regularly raided each other.

One of the palaces in Tikal. Picture by Dennis Jarvis.

The Mayan Collapse has fascinated Westerners since the ruins were first discovered and described by 19th century European visitors. The modern-day obsession with "mysterious sites," evidenced by a raft of dubious documentaries and spurious scholarship attributing Mayan triumphs to everyone from aliens to Atlantis, has obscured the fact that recent scholarship has done much to clear up not only the details of the dynastic struggles of the Maya but also the reasons for the eventual collapse of their civilization. In fact, there is nothing shocking about the idea that an entire cultural area can suffer an irretrievable collapse, as history offers plenty of examples. In his book on the subject, *Collapse, How Societies Choose to Fail or Succeed*, Jared Diamond examined not only the Maya but also Easter Island, the Pitcairn Islands, the Anasazi, the Vikings in Greenland, and contemporary China, Australia and Hispaniola.

---

49 Martin and Grube (2000), Pg 53

In his book, Diamond argues that the Mayan Collapse was a gradual ecological development brought about by the political and economic systems of Tikal and other cities. Mayan agriculture was heavily dependent upon corn, a relatively protein-poor food (compared to wheat and barley), and they lacked access to a wide selection of domesticated animals, since they only had access to dogs and turkeys. This production was significantly lower in the Maya area than in other parts of Mesoamerica because of poor soils and humid climate. Humidity prevented storing corn for more than a season, the lack of draft animals meant that food could not be transported long distances, and agriculture was labor intensive[50].

As the population levels peaked in the Late Classic period, the time of Tikal's second zenith around the 700s, Mayan farmers were exploiting increasingly precarious farmlands, leading to deforestation and erosion on an unprecedented scale. Even the glorious buildings in the center of Tikal would have needed immense amounts of wood to make the thick layers of plaster that covered the surfaces. In turn, this may have led to human-produced droughts caused by the disruptions to water cycles, all due to lack of forests and the speed of runoff without the entrapment caused by roots. Furthermore, in 760 AD, the worst regional drought in thousands of years began, lasting over four decades and exacerbating all of these problems As eroded farmland was abandoned and drought spread, there would have been increasing conflicts amongst farmers and growing anger at the ruling class that was not performing its role as intercessors with the divine. In fact, in the city of Copán, that anger would turn to outright violence; the royal palace was burned to the ground in 850 AD, and nothing was heard from the elites after that.[51]

The Collapse affected a wide range of Classical cities, including Tikal, Calakmul, Palenque and Caracol, but it did not affect all of the Maya. This was especially true of those in the far north of the Yucatan Peninsula, who would found new cities like Uxmal, Chichén Itzá and Mayapán in the wake of the Collapse. Moreover, the Maya themselves around Tikal did not disappear. In fact, they live there still, making up the majority of the population of northern Guatemala and surrounding Mexican states. Instead, the Collapse should be understood as a political event: the collapse of the traditional Mayan dynastic system and the loss of much of the Mayan population in the resulting famines.

What did the Collapse look like? It was a slow-moving event, affecting peripheral areas first and the great heartlands later. Famine and drought would have driven peasants from marginal lands, filling the cities with beggars and swelling recruits to armies. Some families would march far away to the north in search of new lands, founding Yucatecan cities like Uxmal. At the same time, rival kings would have sought to take advantage of weaker rivals or expand their weakening agricultural base at their enemies' expense. Increasingly desperate armies likely came to resemble bandits, and their kings probably acted more like bandit captains. People may have turned to religion and then turned against it, desecrating temples and burning palaces, killing kings and priests. The population shrunk, not only from outright deaths from starvation, disease and war, but because in desperate and uncertain times when the world seemed to be falling apart, they likely had fewer children[52]. Those that did survive to carry on left the

---

50 *Collapse: How Societies Choose to Fail or Succeed* (2005) by Jared Diamond. Pgs 164-5
51 *ibid* pgs 169-170
52 A modern example of this would be the massive population decline in the former Soviet Union states after the collapse of that government.

cities to avoid all the troubles, and in the process, Tikal and its rivals were ultimately reduced to ruins. When thinking about the Maya Collapse, many descriptions might come to mind, such as "tragic," "fascinating," and even "inevitable", but "enigmatic" and "mysterious" are not among them.

At the same time, it's clear that Tikal influenced later Mayan settlements. Besides its direct role in dominating the political and economic structure of the Mayan heartland during its periods of regional hegemony, Tikal had a much larger place in Mayan history as one of the fonts of the more sophisticated elements of Mayan culture. The first of these was serving as a political role model far beyond the areas it controlled. At its height, other Mayan cities' rulers took great pains to demonstrate their genealogical and ideological links to Tikal, even emulating the city's royal ceremony and regalia. This was especially true after the Teotihuacano Entrada, when the dynastic system was infused with the patriarchal systems and religious rituals and symbolism of Central Mexico. Even after the Collapse of Classical Mayan civilization, it seems that refugees who came to the northern Yucatan also brought this dynastic tradition (albeit with many changes) when they founded new cities like Uxmal, Chichén Itzá and Mayapán[53].

Furthermore, scribes in Tikal were at the forefront in transforming the incipient writing system they inherited from El Mirador and Nakbé into a sophisticated, fully-formed orthography capable of expressing all of the subtleties of human language. This remarkable feat - the creation of writing - has only been accomplished three times in human history: in Mesoamerica, Mesopotamia and China. The beautiful Mayan glyphs reached their fullest flower in Tikal and its neighboring cities, and even today, over 7,000 texts of varying length survive[54].

Chapter 7: Modern Tikal

"The imagination reels. There are reliefs, pyramids, temples in the extinguished city. The damp murmur of the arroyos, voices, crepitations of the intertangling vines, the sound of flapping wings, trickle into the immense sea of silence. Everything palpitates, breathes, exhausting itself in green above the vast roof of Peten." - Miguel Ángel Asturias (1967 Nobel Laureate), in *The Mirror of Lida Sal: Tales Based on Mayan Myths & Guatemalan Legends*, p. 13-14.

The city of Tikal was abandoned, but it was never truly lost or forgotten. When the Spanish arrived in the Lake Peten Itzá area in the 1620s, they found the local Itzá Maya rulers from the nearby lake city of Tayasal worshiping at the ruins and venerating its builders, well aware that ancient Tikal's people were their ancestors[55]. In the Colonial period, it was occasionally visited by Spaniards and was certainly well-known by local hunters who regularly traveled through it on their treks.

The first Guatemalan government survey of the ruins was done in 1848, and this was followed by Eusebio Lara's drawings of stelae on the site, which attracted considerable attention. While Guatemala declared its independence in 1825, it was not until 1840 that it was fully independent of the United Provinces of Central America. Since the very beginning, Guatemala has sought to establish its national

---

53 Pohl (1999), pg 73
54 Pohl (1999), pg67
55 Pohl (1999) pg 69

identity based in part upon a glorification of the ancient Mayan past, which is deeply troubling considering the great lengths that this same government has gone to keep down the Mayan peoples actually living in its territory, even to the point of an attempted genocide in the late 20th century. Despite these contradictions, the Guatemalan government has based much of its symbolism upon the Maya, including a Classical sculpture of a Mayan head on the 25 centavo coin and Tikal's Temple I on the back of the old 1/2 Quetzal note. [56]

In 1877, Europeans became increasingly interested in Tikal and the other ruins, especially after Austrian national Gustav Bernoulli visited the city and took a series of wood carved panels back home with him[57]. These panels, which were from Temples I and IV depicted, the life of Jasaw Chan K'awiil I, and while their plunder and movement to museums in Austria was certainly a theft from the Guatemalan people, it allowed the fragile wood to be preserved to the modern day. After Bernoulli, there were other expeditions. In 1881 and 1882 the English proto-archaeologist Alfred Maudslay made a map and survey of the city, and Teobert Maler took photos for the Peabody Museum[58]. From 1926-1937, Sylvanus Morley from Harvard University and the Carnegie Institute made surveys, and there has been an almost continuous period of work at Tikal since, including an elaborate 18 year project by the Guatemalan Government and the University of Pennsylvania[59].

In 1979, the site was given recognition by the United Nations Education, Science and Cultural Organization (UNESCO) as a "World Heritage Site"[60]. It did so on a number of overarching criteria that capture some of the ruins' importance to humanity; Tikal was selected "to represent a masterpiece of human creative genius; to bear a unique or at least exceptional testimony to a cultural tradition or to a civilization which is living or which has disappeared; to be an outstanding example of a type of building, architectural or technological ensemble or landscape which illustrates (a) significant stage(s) in human history…"

The site's ecological value, preserving a wide swath of forest as it does, is also recognized by UNESCO. In this regard, Tikal was selected "to be outstanding examples representing significant on-going ecological and biological processes in the evolution and development of terrestrial, fresh water, coastal and marine ecosystems and communities of plants and animals; to contain the most important and significant natural habitats for in-situ conservation of biological diversity, including those containing threatened species of outstanding universal value from the point of view of science or conservation."

Of course, Tikal is not simply a site of research or international recognition but also a premier tourist site today. Thousands of tourists come annually to marvel over the ruins of the once mighty city, helping ensure that the world's fascination with the Ancient Maya doesn't end anytime soon.

---

56 The Guatemalan currency is the "Quetzal".
57 An image of the panels can be seen here: http://www.allposters.com/-sp/A-Carved-Wood-Lintel-from-Temple-IV-at-Tikal-Collected-in-1877-by-the-Explorer-Gustav-Bernoulli-Posters_i10133629_.htm
58 Pohl (1999) pg 70
59 For a reconstruction of Tikal based upon Penn's work, visit: http://www.penn.museum/sites/expedition/rebuilding-the-ruins/
60 "Tikal" at the World Heritage Site Homepage, accessed online at: whc.unesco.org/en/list/64

Uxmal

Chapter 1: Description of the Site

A picture of the front of the Governor's Palace

"We took another road, and, emerging suddenly from the woods, to my astonishment came at once upon a large open field strewed with mounds of ruins, and vast buildings on terraces, and pyramidal structures, grand and in good preservation, richly ornamented, without a bush to obstruct the view, and in picturesque effect almost equal to the ruins of Thebes...The place of which I am now speaking was beyond all doubt once a large, populous, and highly civilized city. Who built it, why is was located away from water or any of those natural advantages which have determined the sites of cities whose histories are known, what led to its abandonment and destruction, no man can tell." - John Lloyd Stephens, *Incidents of Travel in Central America, Chiapas & Yucatán*, 1843[61]

The city of Uxmal, which once housed an estimated 20,000 people in its urban core and many thousands of others in peripheral farms and vassal cities, is the northernmost of the Puuc city-states that thrived for several centuries in the northern Yucatán Peninsula beginning around the 800s. Uxmal is a majestic city even in its modern ruined form, dominating the landscape from its position atop the Puuc and looking out over the great wide plain of the Yucatán jungle. From atop its pyramids, its ancient rulers must have been able to see much of their kingdom.

While Uxmal would eventually be superseded in economic and political might by the lowland cities of Chichén Itzá and Mayapán, it would maintain its stately glory long after the city's arrival on the

---

61 Quoted in: "Uxmal" at *MayanRuins.com* accessed online at: http://mayaruins.com/uxmal01.html

scene and even become a venerated dowager empress to these later cities. Even after its abandonment, the Maya continued to come to its ruins for ceremonial purposes, and their noble families proudly traced their ancestry back to its halls. .

Like all Mayan cities, Uxmal is built around a ceremonial core centered on temples[62], and in Uxmal, this core was built along a north-south axis and was roughly 100,000 square feet (30,000 square meters) in size. The core's social role is comparable to the Westminster area of London: large buildings for administration, housing royals, religious worship and large public gatherings and celebrations[63]. That said, one of the major differences between Uxmal and its southern Classical precursors is that the monumental architecture dominating the city's core is not focused upon the entombment and veneration of dead monarchs but is instead focused upon facilities for the use of the living. In other words, the broad plazas before the tomb-pyramids (such as the central plaza of Tikal) was replaced as the city focal point by grand halls and palaces around central courtyards in Uxmal[64].

The most famous structure in Uxmal is probably the "Pyramid of the Magician," a name that comes from the Spanish "Pirámide del adivino" (which is probably better translated as the Pyramid of the "Diviner" or "Soothsayer"). Rising 115 feet (35 meters), it is crowned by a temple, but unlike all other Mesoamerican pyramids, the base of this structure is elliptical in shape, with the longest measurements of its sides being 280 feet (85 meters) by 165 feet (50 meters).

The Pyramid has five chambers that are traditionally considered to be temples and which archaeologists have numbered using Roman Numerals. Temple V sits at the crown and is called the House of the Magician,[65] and it is known for its impressive latticework panels. Just below it on the structure is Temple IV, which was far more sumptuous in its décor compared to the relative austerity of Temple V. The gate to Temple IV was enormous and covered in zoomorphic masks, geometric patterns and statuary. Since the entrance to Temple V was not visible from the ground, but Temple IV was, it was probable that IV was the central public space of worship[66]. From a distance, as a visitor ascends towards Temple IV, the facade looms above him or her and appears to be the maw of some terrible monster, and it is only when the visitor reaches the top that the complex patterns of statuary and carving separate from one another[67]. This face has been argued to be the creator god Itzamna[68], who is sometimes depicted as a great serpent[69].

62 A three dimensional tour of the reconstructed ruins can be found here: http://www.uxmal-3d.com/
63 Pohl (1999). Pgs 108 - 109
64 Pohl (1999). Pg 106
65 These names in Spanish and English were assigned to the sites long after their fall and have no relationship to the original Mayan uses of the sites. The House of the Magician was probably named in a pique of romantic drama as the house seemed to float dramatically above the canopy.
66 For an image of the two entrances visit: http://academic.reed.edu/uxmal/galleries/Mid/Uxmal/Magician/Uxmal-Magician-6.htm
67 Pohl (1999). Pg 110
68 "Uxmal Temple of the Magician" accessed online at: http://inneroptics.net/mayan_kingdom_book/uxmal/
69 "Itzamna" at the Mythology Dictionary (2012). Accessed online at: http://www.mythologydictionary.com/itzamna-mythology.html

Pictures of the Pyramid of the Magician

Map of the layout of the Pyramid of the Magician

As that description suggests, the Pyramid of the Magician demonstrates that Uxmal fused a number of architectural styles as it was seeking its own aesthetic (what would eventually become the Puuc Style, detailed below). The ornate Temple IV is in a more Classical, southern style called Chenes, while the simpler Temple V is in a local Puuc style[70].

To the south of the Pyramid of the Magician is the "Governor's Palace," or the "House of the Governor," which is sometimes considered to be the greatest masterpiece of Mayan architecture. The Palace, which was almost certainly a royal palace, is the largest building in Uxmal and is built on a platform that was located atop another platform (48 feet, 15 meter tall). The Palace is built with a simple, harmonious plan: a long central building flanked by two smaller structures joined to it by roofed arcades. The three buildings share a roof line and are joined together by sharing their raised dais, with a single central staircase.

The compound also had a facade decoration of remarkable contrast. The lower exterior walls, up until a little over the tops of the 13 identical doorways, were covered in smooth, undecorated stucco, but above this is the decorative cornice, a massive carved surface covered in images of ancestors, deities (especially Chaak the rain god), and elaborate geometrical images. Each panel was undoubtedly a work of art comparable to the famous friezes of the Parthenon in Athens (now on display in London). Visitors approaching the central staircase finds these friezes to be particularly impressive because the building has a feature called a "negative batter," meaning that the front walls lean forward. In fact, the base of the facade is close to two feet further from the front staircase than the crest of the frieze. The effect of this carefully planned feature is that the friezes appear to soar overhead, giving additional drama to the structure. The interior of the structure was similarly dramatic, with high vaulted arches

---

70 Pohl (1999). Pg 110

and broad paved rooms[71].

71 Pohl (1999). Pgs 112 - 113

Pictures of the Governor's Palace

In front of the House of the Governor is a broad plaza, and on the far side is a worn stone throne carved in the shape of a two-headed jaguar. If one was to stand in the center of the House of the Governor and look directly toward the throne, in a straight line beyond it would be the main pyramid of the vassal city of Kabah. The two-headed jaguar throne appears to have been a symbol of the city since it appears in stone carvings, including one of the only known king, Lord Chak.

Picture of the stone throne

Pictures of the Great Pyramid

Sculptures atop the temple on the Great Pyramid

The other large structure within the ceremonial center (which has a number of smaller temples, ceremonial ballcourts and elite residential complexes) is called the Nunnery Quadrangle, due to its similarity to a Spanish cloister. This is believed to have been the home of one of the city's elite families and is the grandest of numerous palaces in the city. The complex has four buildings surrounding a central plaza, and it is located almost at the feet of the Pyramid of the Magician. Each of the four buildings is distinct as well. For example, the North is the largest and is 330 feet (100 meters) long and 23 feet (7 meters) high, with friezes that mimic a number of the themes found in the Palace of the Governors. The West building is elaborately decorated with images of the great Central Mexican and Chichén Itzá god Kukulkán the feathered serpent and the earth god Pawahtun. The East building is far less grand but has two-headed serpent carvings, while the friezes of the South building have depictions of miniature houses and mask panels. Archaeologists have argued that the iconography of the North building is associated with the heavens, the West building with the earth, and the South building with the underworld. The East building is still being interpreted[72].

72 Pohl (1999). Pgs 111 - 112

The North Building

The East Building

The South Building and West Building

A feathered serpent engraved on the West Building

While often overlooked by tourists and even many archaeologists, the bulk of the city of Uxmal is found not it the impressive buildings of the ceremonial core but in the residential neighborhoods that sprawl outwards from it. After all, it was here the the vast majority of the citizenry lived and worked, and like all Maya cities, Uxmal was strongly divided between a small elite and a massive laboring class beneath them.

Of course, the residential homes reflect this division. The simplest form of housing was (and in many areas of the rural Yucatán still is) the "pole-and-thatch" style. In this type of home, the builder creates a wooden framework based around four corner poles, and once this framework is in place, outer walls are constructed by lashing horizontal poles between the uprights at the top and bottom and then creating a fence of thin branches between them. The resulting home is only semi-enclosed, so while visitors cannot see in, residents can see out, and breezes waft through the building to keep down the often-oppressive heat. The roof of the home is made of thatching, and the floor of the hut is made of pounded earth which can be easily kept clean by sweeping.

While central buildings like the Pyramid of the Magician or the Governor's Palace were most certainly planned formally by professional architects, the vernacular architecture of the common Maya home was built in a more piecemeal fashion. Generally speaking, buildings were constructed around a central courtyard that included space for gardens, perhaps pens for turkeys, a cistern full of wáter, and outbuildings like a kitchen (separated to prevent losses from cooking fires and to keep the main home cool) and a washroom (the Maya are fastidiously clean and sometimes bath several times a day). As the extended family grew, new rooms might be added to the perimeter of the courtyard, including separate sleeping rooms for unmarried children, new bedrooms for recently-married couples, and other storage rooms. Pole-and-thatch would eventually be replaced if the family had enough wealth to build stone walls, so a family compound may have a combination of wooden and stone buildings.

As might be expected, the stuccoed white stone homes had several advantages over their wooden predecessors. Among other advantages, they did not blow away during the periodic hurricanes, they were safer from thieves, they remained cooler than the outside, and they were a symbol of the family's status. That said, even within stone construction, there was a wide variety of stones of varying qualities, as well as a wide range in proficiency among the carvers and masons, meaning that not all stone construction was equally prestigious. As a result, it was possible for very wealthy individuals to demonstrate their status through the construction of stunning buildings made of exceptional stone, both in size and level of quality[73].

Even the homes of elites had a number of similarities to those of the commoners. As was described above in the Nunnery Quadrangle, the wealthy also had homes built around central courtyards with numerous rooms facing inwards, but of course, the Nunnery also demonstrated the differences between common housing and the finest of the Uxmal palaces. For example, the Nunnery had paved floors both within the houses and in the courtyard itself, as well as a prestigious raised platform or terrace upon which the entire complex was constructed, stone roofs with vaulted arches, and elaborately decorated exteriors and interiors. Where the commoners' homes enjoyed both privacy from the exterior and the ability to look out through the loosely woven walls, the elites achieved the same effect by having stonecarvers make them elaborate limestone latticework for their walls. These elites put great effort into their homes, which appear not only to be constructed for comfort but also to be able to both host and inspire awe in large numbers of guests. The ruling class' culture in Uxmal under the rule of their council appears to have become a world of sophisticated courtly intrigue involving rival families and a need to entertain on a grand scale. The grandees of Renaissance Venice would have instantly recognized the interplay between politics and socialization that played out in these grand homes.

Chapter 2: Daily Life in Uxmal

After exploring the ruined homes of commoners and elites, visitors are left with all kinds of burning

---

73 "People who Lived in Stone Houses: Local Knowledge and Social Difference in the Classic Maya Pucc Region of Yucatan, Mexico" by Kelli Carmean, Patricia A. McAnany and Jeremy A. Sabloff (2011). In the journal *Latin American Antiquity* Vo 22, No 2, Pp 143 - 158

questions. What was daily life like for these people? How did they go about the events, big and small, that marked their lives? Archaeology can tell visitors much about architecture and provide insights into economic life, but it often stumbles when faced with more intangible questions and figuring out some of the more fragile parts of material life, such as clothing and food. To determine answers, scholars must supplement archaeological data with information from colonial and other written sources who recorded daily life in the Yucatán, but since these documents are necessarily several centuries older than the apex of Uxmal's influence in the late 800s, they also have to be taken with a grain of salt.

Mayan elites, from the days of the Classical cities all the way down tot he arrival of the Spanish, delighted in adorning themselves in spectacular costumes, at least for ceremonial occasions. Early in the Classical Period, a royal "costume" was created, and it remained remarkably stable over the centuries, which in some sense is not surprising since European monarchs' ceremonial outfits have also not significantly altered in centuries and are in turn based off of models from the Roman Empire. The only good image of a monarch in Uxmal is of the famed Lord Chak on stela 14 (which is also discussed further below). In this image, he is dressed as a traditional Classical monarch, with an elaborate feathered headdress, a straight piercing through his nose, decorative plates in his ears, a collar made of jade, embroidered loincloth, and relatively simple sandals.[74] This shows that despite the dramatic changes the leaders of Uxmal made to their political system over time, they still maintained at least a symbolic connection to the ritual life of the Classical Maya courts.

---

74 Detail of Stela 14 can be found here:
https://www.peabody.harvard.edu/CMHI/detail.php?num=14&site=Uxmal&type=Stela#

A depiction of Lord Chak

Stela 14

Outside of this very specific costume, clothing was probably quite simple, and the Spanish missionary Diego de Landa described the peasants as wearing clothing well-suited to the muggy climate of the region. Men wore a breechcloth, which consisted of a strip of cotton passing between the legs and pulled up through a cotton belt so that the ends dangled down in front of the groin and covered the buttocks. Mayan women (then and now) wore *huipil* - simple cotton gowns[75] - and square cotton mantles with holes cut in the center. On their feet, both genders and all social classes from the king down wore sandals made of deerskin or hemp with a thong between the toes.[76]

75 "The Huipil" at *Images of the Maya*. Accessed online at: http://www.flmnh.ufl.edu/maya/maya5.htm
76 *Yucatan Before and After the Conquest* by Friar Diego de Landa. William Gates (trans.) 1566 (1978). Dover Books. Pgs 33, 53-54

Naturally, while clothing types were fairly uniform, there was plenty of variations and different styles. To begin with, the cotton garments - the breechcloths, huipils and mantles - were often elaborately decorated with embroidery, and the breechcloths could be adorned with colorful feathers that were also valuable trade goods. Elites adorned themselves with elaborate jewelry of jade, turquoise, shell and metal.

In addition to the relatively simple clothing, the people engaged in a number of forms of body modification for the purposes of beauty, including tattoos, filed teeth, piercings (especially of the nasal septum and the ears), and "coiffures as fine as those of the most coquettish Spanish women."[77] In addition to de Landa's rich descriptions, scholars can confirm these details thanks to fresco paintings from the walls of the ruins, carvings of both lordly individuals and their servitors on Stone, and a handful of painted paper books.

Clothing may have served an additional purpose beyond demonstrating one's good taste and social class (or lack thereof). For example, it may have also indicated one's place of origin. In the grand Guatemalan Maya market town of Chichicastenango, and even today in each of the surrounding Maya vilages, the women possess a style of huipil decoration that is unique to that community, marking individuals when they come to mix in the central community (as they would have in the markets of Uxmal).[78]

These markets would have been one of the primary reasons for the existence of Uxmal, in addition to its religious and political roles. Archaeologists have discovered that by the time of the founding of Uxmal, the Maya region had already been tied into a massive trade network for centuries. To the south, it extended into the rainforests of modern-day Honduras, but to the north it stretched all the way through today's Mexico into the American states of Arizona, New Mexico, Texas, and even Colorado and Utah. Long-distance trade goods that regularly passed hands included cotton, salt, cacao beans, jade, turquoise, polished silver mirrors, copper bells, seashells, colorful feathers, fine stone tools, and exceptional pottery. Locally, Uxmal would have served as the nexus for a much more localized network that brought goods in from the nearby farms and forests, including corn, beans, squash, chilis, fruit, wild game, turkeys, wild honey and wax, wood for fires and buildings, and other building materials[79]. The diet in Uxmal would have been heavy in corn, especially in the form of omnipresent tortillas, and relatively poor in protein despite the consumption of beans and wild game (especially deer)[80].

The Maya did not have permanent markets like the bazaars and souqs of the Muslim world, but it appears that markets were regularly organized by urban elites in central plazas. In fact, the Maya word for plaza, k'iwik, is also the term used for a marketplace. Vendors, both local and long-distance, would have gathered in these central places and paid a fee to the city administration, and in turn, these fees

77 de Landa 1566 (1978). Pgs 33, 53-54
78 *Chichicastenango: A Guatemalan Village* by Ruth Leah Bunzel (1967). University of Washington Press.
79 "Mesoamerican Plants and Foods" accessed online at:
   http://clio.missouristate.edu/chuchiak/New%20Webpage%20Images/HST%20397---Theme%205---Mesoamerican_plants_and_foods.htm
80 de Landa 1566 (1978). Pgs 32-39, 93-101

and the tribute that elites took from their landholdings in surrounding communities formed the backbone of the elaborate elite lifestyle.

As the city grew in importance, the leaders increasingly connected it to surrounding communities via raised highways. Both the marketplaces and the highways were increasingly more extensive and formalized by the period of Uxmal's dominance over the region, prefiguring the continent-spanning trade network of Chichén Itzá.[81] Unlike Chichén Itzá, which would specialize in the export of first salt and then cotton, economic life in the city of Uxmal was not so specialized; instead, it tended to import primarily goods for elite consumption and a few for practical uses. For instance, obsidian for tools was probably imported in a raw form and then locally shaped to meet the needs of customers. Uxmal also served as a spot for redistribution, and its exports were most likely of the generalized southern Mesoamerican variety, including colorful feathers, cotton, and cacao.

Chapter 3: Origins of the City

Picture of a facade referred to as the Patio of the Birds

81 "The Elusive Maya Marketplace: An Archaeological Consideration of the Evidence" by Leslie C. Shaw (2012) in *The Journal of Archaeological Research* January 2012. Accessed online at: http://link.springer.com.libezproxy2.syr.edu/article/10.1007/s10814-011-9055-0/fulltext.html

Picture of the House of the Doves taken from the Great Pyramid

Mayan civilization did not originate in Uxmal or anywhere near the now-venerable city. Instead, the Mayan peoples originated in the south, in the region that is now known as the Highlands of Guatemala, Belize and the Mexican states of Chiapas and Campeche. These wet and mountainous lands gave birth to a collection of complex, large, and perpetually feuding city-states like Tikal, Caracol, Calakmul and Palenque. The inhabitants of these cities, known as the Classic Maya people, thrived from roughly 200-800 AD, and they built mighty temples and established elaborate mythology, astronomy, architecture, irrigation and other arts and sciences[82].

However, by the 700s, the Classical Mayan society was beginning to suffer an ecological, political and demographic decline. Agriculture had always been relatively precarious, if only because their central staple of corn (maize) is por in proteins compared to other cereals and they had few domesticated animals to supplement their diet. Furthermore, humidity prevented easy storage of corn from season to season. When the Mayan populations peaked in the early 700s, desperate peasant farmers began cutting down hillside forests to grow more crops, but that led to widespread erosion and

82 *The Atlas of World Archaeology* by Paul G. Bahn (ed.) (2009). The Brown Reference Group Ltd. Pgs 170-171.

flooding. In 760, a devastating four decade-long drought hit the region, wiping out the food supply for all of the marginalized populations clinging to the hillsides. Exactly how this collapse occurred varied from place to place, but it would have been a gradual affair that witnessed the abandonment of eroded farms, the flooding of cities with beggars and work-seekers, and increasingly desperate monarchies starting wars over resources with their neighbors. Of course, the warfare would've led to more poor people in the cities in the form of refugees. Finally, there were urban revolts such as the one in 850 in Copan, where the royal palace was burnt. The political order then crumbled into bandit-kings pretending to be monarchs, and they would've been ruling over crumbling cities that suffered from widespread starvation, declining birthrates, shortened lifespans, and overall decline.[83]

Thanks to at least some if not all these factors, sometime in the 8th century AD, groups of farmers from the mountainous heartland of Mayan civilization began to slowly migrate north into the Yucatán Peninsula between the modern cities of Mérida and Cancún as they fled the crumbling kingdoms. Unlike the mighty dynasties of the great city-states that they left, noone felt the need to write about these people, perhaps because they were most likely economic or political refugees escaping the slow-moving crisis of the Classical Collapse. Their descendants today still live in the Yucatán and speak a language called Yucatecan Mayan, whose closest cousin is a relatively obscure Mayan language called Lacandón, which in turn is spoken by some of the poorest and most marginalized Mayan peasants living in today's state of Chiapas near the ruins of the Classical cities of Bonampak, Yaxchilan and Palenque[84]. Hence, one might suspect that at least the first or most numerous of the migrants heading north and carving settlements out of the Yucatán Jungle would have originated in this corner of the Mayan Highlands. Certainly, their agricultural experiences in the similar landscape of the Lacandon Jungle would have at least given them the hope that they might survive in their new homes.

Anyone seeking the originators of Uxmal and the entire Yucatecan Mayan cultural tradition (including the cities of Mayapán and Chichén Itzá) should look first to these humble migrants, who probably moved in groups larger than a single family. While one must be careful comparing groups spread across almost a thousand years, Mayans in both the Yucatán and Lacandon regions have demonstrated a remarkable sense of community spirit, including migrating as whole villages to escape oppressive governments[85], fighting guerilla wars in both the 19th and 20th centuries[86], and founding a region of semi-independent "Autonomous Villages" completely free of government control during the Zapatista Revolt from 1992 to today[87]. Thus, while it can never be said for certain, it is probable that villages of peasants from the scarred and dying landscape around Palenque and Yaxchilan decided in their village councils to leave the rule of the Classical dynastic kings and to move to a harsh land to the north to settle new villages. Given enough time, they may have sent scouts ahead to find potential

83 *Collapse: How Societies Choose to Fail or Succeed* (2005) by Jared Diamond. Pgs 164-5
84 "Maya, Yucatec" and "Lacandon" at the *Ethnologue, Languages of the World* website. Accessed online at: http://www.ethnologue.com/language/yua and http://www.ethnologue.com/language/lac.
85 Such as the village of Cobá described in: *Life Under the Tropical Canopy: Tradition and Change Among the Yucatec Maya* by Ellen Kintz (1990). Case Studies in Cultural Anthropology.
86 Especially the recent Zapatista Revolution and the brutal Caste War of 1847-1855: *The Caste War of the Yucatán* by Nelson A. Reed (2001). Stanford University Press.
87 *Mayan Lives, Mayan Utopias: The Indigenous Peoples of Chiapas and the Zapatista Rebellion* by Jan Rus, Rosalva Aida Hernandez Castillo and Shannan L. Mattiace (eds.) (2003). Rowman and Littlefield.

places to inhabit, or perhaps their decisions were made in a time of immediate crisis without the luxury of caution, but either way, they packed up their possessions in the 7th and 8th centuries and dropped out of the official Mayan written histories of the day, at least for a time.

What did they encounter as they moved north? While the Yucatán appears to the casual observer to be a lush rainforest covered in a thick, green forest cover, Mayan farmers would've considered the terrain to be as challenging and intimidating as a desert. If anything, it can be thought of as a "Green Desert" because it has little rainfall and almost no surface bodies of water. On top of that, the entire Yucatán Peninsula is a great sheet of limestone, so the water that does fall is either absorbed by plants or drains away immediately into the porous, cave-filled rocks under the thin soils. This landscape is known by geologists as a "karst topography." Like most rainforests, the soils of the Yucatán were poor because most of the nutrients were locked up within the trees themselves. Accustomed to the terraces and irrigated landscapes of the south, this Green Desert would have been as intimating to the migrants as any desert of sand and rock.

Eventually, the descendants of these migrants would spread out across the lowlands and found great cities on the limestone shelf, but the first migrants would have only been able to settle these regions in small, scattered groups. In the beginning, they had no way of yet knowing how to extract water from the underground sinkholes called cenotes, and it probably took several generations to breed new strains of corn and other crops more tolerant to the hostile conditions.

As a result, this first wave of inhabitants settled in the only area of notable topographic relief in the entire region: a line of low rises called the Puuc Hills. The term "Puuc" is derived from the Mayan word for a mountain ridge, and the region sprawls over 4,700 square miles (7,500 square kilometers). In the Puuc Region, they found grottoes, which were former sinkholes that had partially collapsed and thereby created open waterholes. These would later be supplemented by cutting cisterns called chultunes into the limestone rock. In this location, the settlers were able to recreate their dense southern villages, which would eventually become the nucleus of new cities, the most important of which would become Uxmal. The agricultural importance of the region would remain for centuries, and even the Spanish refered to it as the "granary" of their colony since it produced two crops of corn a year[88].

---

88 Pohl (1999). Pgs 105 - 108

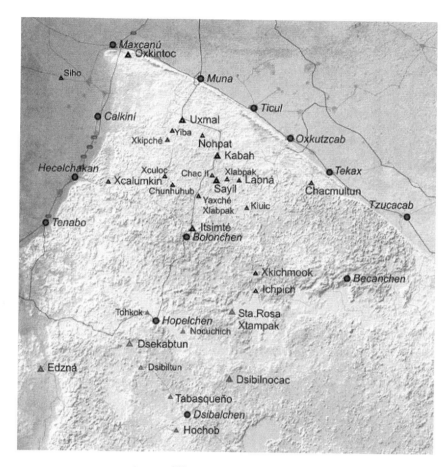

A map of Mayan sites in the Puuc region

It seems strange to many modern observers and scholars that the south collapsed while the north did not, especially considering the fact that agriculture in the south was richer and more stable than in the north. However, it was in the places where urban life was the most stable, the oldest, and the most secure that the collapse occurred. Meanwhile, in the frontier cities of the Puuc region - Uxmal foremost among them - Mayan urban life continued unabated for centuries to come. How can anyone explain this apparent paradox of famine in the rich lands and survival (if not feast) in the poor ones? In his book *Collapse: How Societies Choose to Fail or Succeed*, author Jared Diamond took up just this question, and he asserted that there are a number of causes. The first is that populations were much denser in the old kingdoms of the south, so farmers were forced to use even the most marginal of lands for the their crops, making them particularly susceptible to crop failure. Furthermore, the southern lands - unlike the Yucatán - had very deep water tables, making well-drilling impractical.[89] At the same time, the economies of these cities were largely isolated from easy water transport since they were in the Highlands, and trade was specialized around importing elite goods for the glorification of the dynastic system. The Yucatán, on the other hand, was not bound to the Dynastic system and was close to trade routes (especially the ascendent Chichén Itzá), and furthermore, the people here were willing to export bulk goods and import food during times of crisis. Together, these circumstances allowed the young Puuc cities to weather the storm of the Maya Collapse.

Chapter 4: The Puuc Era

If a casual reader should learn anything about Uxmal compared to other Mayan ruins, it is that Uxmal was the creator and pinnacle of the uniquely Puuc Style. The Puuc style is definitely a Mayan form of architecture, but it changed many of the earlier techniques and assumptions. As discussed earlier, the city's emphasis moved from veneration of royal tombs in the Classical tradition to the creation of palaces for the living in the Puuc Style. Another major change was in decoration itself. Both northern and southern traditions involved the creation of elaborate facades, but while in the south these facades were constructed by shaping stucco on bare rock, in Uxmal (and its imitators), the facades were created by having artisans shape thousands of small geometric stole tiles that were then affixed to the exterior of the buildings, thus creating elaborate patterns[90].

---

89 Diamond (2005). Pgs 157 - 177
90 Pohl (1999). Pg 106

Mosaic-like decorations on the Nunnery Quadrangle

Puuc buildings were defined by having facades divided into plain, smooth lower portions and elaborately decorated friezes. These friezes were decorated with both geometric motifs but also masks of deities, especially the rain god Chak. In addition to Uxmal, where the style reached its pinnacle in the House of the Governor, it was also present in nearby Puuc cities like Kabah, Labna, and Sayil. The style is also present in the older areas of Chichén Itzá, such as the Nunnery Annex (no connection to the Nunnery Quadrangle in Uxmal) and the early forms of the Castillo pyramid[91].

A strong argument can be made that one of the ways that Uxmal broke most impressively from the Classical Tradition was its rejection of Dynasticism. Unlike its southern predecessors, which Uxmal copied so diligently in other matters, Uxmal did not maintain monuments designed to elevate and venerate a ruling dynasty; there are no great temples to royal lines (like the North Acropolis of Tikal) or elaborate carved stelae detailing royal pedigrees and the acts of kings. The House of the Governor was apparently a place of government, but it was not a royal palace, and the city had a number of elite compounds that must have been inhabited by rival families. This rule by council was referred to later during the League of the Mayapán and early Colonial period as "Mul Tepal" ("joint rule"). Officially, the city records do note a founder of the city, Hun-Uitzil-Chac, but nothing else is known about him besides his name, and it may be that he was created by elite families at a much later date[92].

There is some echo of this Mul Tepal system at Uxmal in a folktale recorded in the 19th century and known as the "Legend of the Dwarf." The story goes that an old woman hatched a magical egg and found a baby human within, but the child never grew to adult size and instead remained a dwarf. Dwarves hold a special place in Mesoamerican myth as figures blending the boundary between the human and supernatural worlds, so the adopted mother of this dwarf insisted that he should become king. The dwarf was forced into a physical challenge against the king, but when the dwarf triumphed, the angry sovereign insisted that the dwarf build the mightiest structure in the city overnight or be put to death. The next morning, the city was awed by the construction of the Pyramid of the Magician (also called the Pyramid of the Dwarf). The dwarf then killed the king and ascended to the throne.[93]

While the Pyramid of the Magician was definitely not built overnight and was constructed in a series of ever-greater stages, the story may explain the struggles for power in the great city. In the Classic Mayan city-state, the very idea that someone could challenge the king for his throne was never considered, and while there were certainly struggles, they were between members of existing dynastic lines and were never formalized or ritualized. In Uxmal, however, there may have been something like a confederation of elite families who competed for the rulership position. This was not a Classical royal tradition but may have emerged out of the more humble roots of Uxmal and other Puuc

---

91 "Uxmal" at the *Encyclopedia Britannic Online*. Accessed online at:
http://www.britannica.com/EBchecked/topic/620988/Uxmal#ref225522
92 "Lords of the Northern Maya: Dynastic History in the Inscriptions of Uxmal and Chichén Itza" by Jeff Karl Kowalski in *Expedition Magazine*. Vol 27 No 3 November 1985. Accessed online at:
http://www.penn.museum/sites/expedition/lords-of-the-northern-maya/
93 The tale is recounted at greater length in: *The Myths of Mexico and Peru* by Lewis Spence. 1913 (2005). Barnes and Noble Books. Pgs 167 - 168

settlements, and the relative egalitarianism of the peasant communities from which they came.

That said, by the time Uxmal became a proper city, any signs of this egalitarianism were purely vestigial. Instead, it may have been that Uxmal from the 750s on could be compared to the Roman Republic under the early Caesars: officially a republic with a nod towards the common citizenry, but in practice an elected monarchy dominated by the powerful elite patricians in the capital city.

From this period of glory and power emerges a single name. In fact, it is the only name of a monarch at Uxmal (aside from the name of the founder) that has survived in the written record: Chan Chak K'ak'nal Ajaw, more commonly referred to in the modern era as "Lord Chak." Lord Chak ascended to the double-headed jaguar throne of Uxmal (in fact, scholars have found an image of him atop the throne) in approximately 875 and ruled until 910. Under Lord Chak, the city rose from being one of many amongst the rival hill towns of the Puuc to the undisputed, preeminent political power. During this period, the current forms of both the Nunnery Quadrangle and the Temple of the Magician were created, and the House of the Governor and main ballcourt were entirely constructed. Based off of inscriptions in other settlements, it appears that Lord Chak led his city's armies to victory as well, including conquering neighboring Kabah and constructing an impressive 11 kilometer highway connecting the two.

Another surviving inscription notes his ancestry. According to that record, Lord Chaak Uinal Kan and Lady "Bone" were his parents, but there is no indication either way as to whether Lord Chaak Uinal Kan also held the double-headed jaguar throne. It may be that his mother came from a noble family in Chichén Itzá (which was on the rise in this period) as there is an allusion to that city in conjunction with her name, but its exact meaning is obscure. That said, alliances cemented by marriage in this way were not uncommon amongst elites and it may have been one of the reasons why he was able to consolidate power[94].

Lord Chak's reign is significant not only for Uxmal - it was undoubtedly the moment of greatest glory for the city - but for the Mayan world in general. By the time of his death in 910 AD, all of the great Classical cities had fallen. The last monument was erected in Tikal in 889 AD, the royal palace of Copan was burned in 850 AD, Dos Pilas had been turned into an armed camp for a bandit lord, and Palenque had been quiet for over a century[95]. The stelae erected to commemorate Lord Chak are the very last monuments to a true Classic Maya King, so his death serves as the end of the Classic Era. Of course, that's not to say Uxmal disappeared, but it did become subservient for an extended period of time as it lived within the shadow of Chichén Itzá to the north. The last construction within the ceremonial center of Uxmal was finished by 925 AD.[96]

The seeming lack of kings in the record for Uxmal has led some to believe that the city was actually ruled by its most commonly depicted figure: the rain god Chaac (also spelled Chaak, Chac, and Chak).

94 Kowalski (1985)

95 For more on the Collapse from a southern perspective, consult *Tikal: The History of the Ancient Maya's Famous Capital* by Jesse Harasta (2014). Charles Rivers Editors.

96 *The Chronicle of the Mayan Kings and Queens: Deciphering the Dynasties of the Ancient Maya* by Simon Martin and Nikolai Grube (2000). Thames and Hudson. Pgs 227

In fact, it's imposible to discuss the Puuc style without referring to the omnipresent Chaac masks dotting horizontal surfaces, and the god's image is quite distinctive; he has "goggle" eyes, a proboscus-like nose and often a gaping toothy maw for a mouth[97].

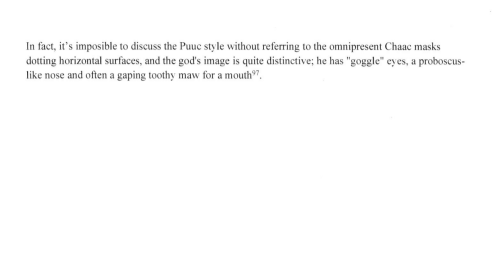

---

97 For example: http://www.flickr.com/photos/tom_martin/4151711134/

Effigy urn in the form of
Chac, the Rain God

A figurine depicting Chaac

Chaac is an old god that was brought up to the Yucatán with the earliest migrants, but the origins of the deity during the Classic Era are up for debate. It has been argued that Chaac was originally brought to the Mayan lands by invaders from Teotihuacán near what is today Mexico City. Teotihuacán conquered Tikal and other Highland cities in the 4th century, and the city worshipped a similar god named Tlaloc. In turn, Tlaloc may have come from a fang-mouthed, wide-eyed rain deity called the "Baby Jaguar" by archaeologists and worshiped among the Olmec people of Veracruz as early as 1500 BC[98]. Chaac was therefore a god of antiquity who held powerful resonance with the Maya by the time they built the city of Uxmal, and it is not surprising in a city whose agriculture depended so much upon regular rainfall (and in a region experiencing prolonged drought) that they would make this deity preeminent in their religious rites.[99]

Chapter 5: Chichén Itzá and the Eclipse of Uxmal

Uxmal's time at the top was relatively short-lived. After the death of Lord Chak, the city was not abandoned like so many of the southern cities, but it went into a long period of inactivity. No new monumental buildings were constructed, no kings were commemorated, and the city does not appear to be mentioned in the inscriptions of its neighbors.

The new power in the region was Chichén Itzá, a lowland city that took advantage of several deep natural wells called cenotes and a monopoly on local salt production. Originally a tiny Mayan statelet surviving in obscurity for several centuries, it was only after the collapse of Classical Mayan society that Chichén Itzá exploded onto the scene. Leveraging its salt production, it was able to command wealthy trade routes connecting it to the Toltec Empire in central Mexico. While Uxmal dominated the central Puuc interior, the Itzaes of Chichén looked outwards to the sea.

It is possible that the two were allies in the early period, as there is evidence that Lord Chak's mother was associated with Chichén, and there is no evidence that Chichén Itzá's rise was accompanied with conflict with Uxmal, a common event when one Mayan city displaced another. Moreover, early buildings in Chichén seem to be modeled after Uxmal. Thus, it's possible that after 925, Uxmal became a sort of junior partner, with its increasingly venerable buildings and its firm dedication to the worship of Chaac[100].

Either way, the situation fundamentally changed in the late 9th century and early 10th century, the period in which the elites of Chichén Itzá adopted cultural traditions imported from the non-Mayan Toltec Empire (located in today's Central Mexico). The most obvious change that can be found today is in the architectural style, because the main Puuc pyramid was covered in a new layer entirely based off of Toltec designs. Chichén Itzá also seems to have imported Toltec warrior societies, a central part

98 *Teotihuacan: The History of Ancient Mesoamerica's Largest City* by Jesse Harasta (2014). Charles Rivers Editors.
99 "Chac" at the *Encyclopedia Mythica* by Henk Jan van Scheicoven (1997). Accessed online at:
   http://www.pantheon.org/articles/c/chac.html and "Chac" at the *Mythology Dictionary* (2012). Accessed online at:
   http://www.mythologydictionary.com/chac-mythology.html
100   *Chichén Itza: The History and Mystery of the Maya's Most Famous City* by Jesse Harasta (2013). Charles Rivers Editors.

of the Toltec state, as well as the worship of the god Kukulcán. There is an alternative theory that the Toltecs conquered the Yucatán, but there is no hard evidence for conquest like there was for Teotihuacan's conquest of Tikal, so it has been largely discarded.[101]

Regardless, thanks to the adoption of Toltec cultural elements, the elites of the newly cosmopolitan system appear to have turned their back on Mayan tradition and instead adopted what may have been viewed as a prestigious international cultura, one associated with exotic goods, wealth, and fascinating new religious ideas. This may have been similar to the ways that European courts far from Paris adopted the French language and culture during the 18th century in order to relate to the standards of international elite high society.

At the heart of the new culture was the cult of the Sovereign Feathered Serpent, a pan-Mesoamerican god called Kukulcán among the Maya and Quetzalcoatl in Central Mexico. Considered to be both a creator deity who protected the world and gave humanity the gift of civilization and also a messianic man who came to Earth and was driven away by a depraved sorcerer, his story resonated all throughout today's Mexico. Its original cultic center was the Toltec capital of Tula, but eventually, Chichén became an alternative center for worship and pilgrimage, making it the heart of the new religion.

A depiction of the deity on El Castillo at Chichén Itzá

There is some evidence of the cult of Kukulcán in Uxmal as well. The feathered serpent appears carved in the friezes of the Nunnery Quadrangle, which was built during the reign of Lord Chak, but

101   "Kukulkan" and "Quetzalcoatl" at the *Encyclopedia Mythica*. Accessed online at: http://www.pantheon.org/. "Kukulcan" at the *Mythology Dictionary*. Accessed online at: http://www.mythologydictionary.com/kukulcan-mythology.html

the deity never had the importance he did at Chichén. Just as Uxmal is the city of Chaac - his face is everywhere and the city's greatest king took his name - Chichén came to be associated with Kukulcán. At the same time, the cult of Chaac appears to have been eclipsed in the hearts of the Maya by the new religion, though this does not mean that the faith in Chaac disappeared entirely. Mayan polytheism allows for the worship of numerous gods, so Chaac may have merely taken a backseat to Kukulcán. At the same time, it's possible that formerly ascendant priests of the rain god were bitter about their new position and sought to knock Kukulcán from his pedestal.

Chapter 6: Revolution and The League of Mayapán

In roughly 1179, the Chichén sister-city of Tula in the Toltec homeland was sacked by invaders from the north, as was the northern port city of el Tajín,[102] which had linked the two. In essence, the trade routes that sustained Chichén power were severed. Already pressured by these losses, the ruling Itzá clan of Chichén Itzá apparently began to apply greater economic pressure on their subject peoples, perhaps to acquire food reserves during crises, perhaps to defend their borders against now-forgotten enemies, or perhaps to just maintain their luxurious lifestyles. The effect, however, was a greater presence of ostensibly foreign and increasingly despised mercenaries in the streets of the city. These "mercenaries" may have been Toltec refugees staying with their fellow co-religionists and members of the same warrior societies, or they may have been literal mercenaries brought in.

Either way, the stage was set for revolt, and the revolution came in the form of a remarkable figure named Hunac Ceel. A military general and presumably member of an elite family from the interior town of Telchaquillo, Hunac Ceel attempted to overthrow the Itzá Dynasty using forces from the inside. His first attempt, probably in the early 1200s, was completely unsuccessful, and after his army was shattered, he was captured. It was determined by the city's leaders, including the ruling Itzá Ah Mex K'uuk, that he should be put to death, so he was sacrificed as an offering to Chaak and thrown into the city's Sacred Cenote well, which was dedicated to the rain god. To everyone's surprise, however, Hunac Ceel emerged alive the next day with prophecies he claimed were from Chaak, and when his prophecies came true, Ah Mex K'uuk (fearing his power) sent him back into the interior to rule over a peripheral town. Hunac Ceel traveled through the old Puuc heartland and gathered strength until he led a second attack on Chichén Itzá. This time he was successful in defeating the Itzaes, and he drove the survivors into present-day Guatemala. After taking out Chichén Itzá, he established a new capital for his revolutionary government (the "League") at the town of Mayapán.[103]

Of course, as the fantastic nature of the story suggests, there is plenty of debate over the actual nature of this revolution. It is tempting to see it as a form of nationalism on the part of the Maya, who finally had the opportunity to overthrow hated foreign rulers and establish a true Mayan government again. Folktales, however, paint a picture of inter-elite strife, so all kinds of alternate theories have been thrown about. Perhaps an unnamed Mayan prince (Hunac Ceel?) was spurned for the hand of the daughter of the ruler of Chichén (Ah Mex K'uuk?), so the prince then led an army that captures his

---

102   The Huaxtecs who had built el Tajín and bridged the Tula-Chichén gap were located in central Mexico but were ethnically and linguistically related to the Maya.

103   "Chapter 2: The Rise of Hunac Ceel to Power" from the *Chilam Balam* accessed online at: http://www.bibliotecapleyades.net/chilam_balam/cbc07.htm

beloved and destroys her home city.

Either way, the inhabitants of Mayapán were able to form an inter-city Mul Tepal (joint rule), with elite families from all of the rebellious cities coming together in council in the new city. Mayapán was therefore not a center of international trade like Chichén had been but instead a planned political capital (akin to modern-day Washington D.C.) with mansions for each of the families for when they came to court. The descendants of Hunac Ceel were known as the Cocom dynasty, and when the Spanish arrived, they still ruled over a small kingdom based around the town of Sotuta between the ruins of Mayapán and Chichén Itza.

The Cocom were not, however, the only prominent family within the League, though they may have had a permanent ceremonial position at its head. At the time of Spanish colonization, the League had broken down and a full 16 petty kingdoms had been formed out of its ruins, so it's possible there had been at least that many powerful families represented at the League. The most important, however, were the Xiu (also called the Tutul Xiu), who were the rulers of Uxmal.

The exact origins of the Xiu are a bit vague, but the family has maintained a genealogical chart since ancient times that claims to include Hun-Uitzil-Chac, the mythical founder of Uxmal. Of course, the fact that they assert this blood connection, while interesting sociologically, hardly confirms its veracity. It's far more likely that this connection was invented by later generations to justify power that they had already seized.[104] What is known is that by the time of Hunac Ceel's rise, the Xiu were firmly in power in Uxmal and that they apparently delivered the city to the League. Their participation, both for material and symbolic purposes, was so crucial that it appears they were granted the status of the League's second family[105].

The new order established by Hunac Ceel and his the Xiu allies appears to not only have displaced Chichén Itza,but also the Toltec-infused cultural order they created. For instance, archaeologists have noted that the previously-popular Toltec style pottery was replaced by self-consciously traditional Mayan styles that had long been out of style.[106] There may have been a religious dimension to this change as well. On the one hand, the worship of Kukulcán did not cease; in fact, the high priest of the god was merely taken from Chichén and moved to a new pyramid at Mayapán (a smaller version of the Castillo pyramid), where he continued to preside as before[107]. At the same time, however, there appears to have been a religious dimension to the revolt since Hunac Ceel received his prophetic visions from Chaak, he traveled to Chaak's city (Uxmal) for support, and there was a general revival of Chaak worship. Unlike the worship of Kukulcán, the worship of Chaak has continued to this day amongst Yucatecan peasants.

Eventually, like the power structures before it, the League was shattered, and the Spanish missionary Diego de Landa described the situation roughly three centuries later: "The governing Cocom began to

104   Kowalski (1985)
105   *Mayapán: History of the Mayan Capital* by Jesse Harasta (2014). Charles Rivers Editors.
106   "Survival and Revival of Terminal Classic Traditions at Postclassic Mayapán" by Susan Milbrath and Carlos Peraza Lope (2009). In the journal *Latin American Antiquity* 20(4) 581-606 accessed online at:
    http://www.jstor.org/discover/10.2307/40650048?uid=3739832&uid=2&uid=4&uid=3739256&sid=21103263281091
107   de Landa 1566 (1978). Pgs 10 - 11

covet riches, and to that end negotiated with the garrison kept by the kings of Mexico in Tabasco and Xicalango, that he would put the city in their charge. In this way he introduced the Mexicans into Mayapán, oppressed the poor and made slaves of many."[108]

This may sound like a repeat of the fall of Chichén, but there are differences. First, Mayapán never dominated the Yucatan economically or religiously in the way that Chichén did; the Cocom may have desired power in the manner that the Itzaes had, but they appear to have always feared for their strength. In addition to possibly using mercenaries, the Cocom built thick walls around Mayapán. No Mayan city had been walled like that before, leading historians to assume that the Cocom felt particularly vulnerable in their capital. This was apparently for good reason, because Landa - who it must be said was a close ally of the Xius - noted that "the lord of the Tutul-xiu never gave his consent to [the mercenaries]... the chiefs then attached themselves to the party of Tutul-xiu, a man patriotic like his ancestors, and they plotted to kill Cocom. This they did, killing at the same time all of his sons save one who was absent...[109]" This probably occurred around 1450 AD.

Perhaps the Xiu had hoped that after the fall of the Cocom, they would be able to ascend to power in the League, but if so, they were sorely disappointed. The League was shattered forever, and the leaders of the revolution soon retreated back to their own seats of power and began warring against one another. Furthermore, it was during this period that Uxmal was finally abandoned. It's not entirely clear why, but all over the northern Yucatan at this point, the great cities were in terminal decline, including Uxmal, Mayapán, and Chichén Itzá. The civil wars may have brought long-distance trade, the lifeblood of many cities, to a halt and may have disrupted local food supplies. Armies may have looted settlements and commoners may have fled to the fortified strongholds of their lords. The fortification of Mayapán may have signified that this internal warring may have begun long before the official collapse of the League.

Whatever the case, the Xiu family left Uxmal to settle in the town of Maní, which was located east of Uxmal in the foothills of the Puuc region. The Xius continued to rule over Uxmal's old heartland, including the city itself, Kabah, Sayil, Labna, and the other ancient Puuc towns[110]. Indeed, the Xiu continued regular religious pilgrimage to Uxmal and recognized it as their ancient seat of power, but the Mayan world had permanently shifted, and Uxmal – while still revered – was never again permanently inhabited.

Chapter 7: The Abandonment and Rediscovery of Uxmal

Uxmal remained revered among the Maya, but everything changed in 1521 when Hernan Cortes landed on the Yucatan peninsula. While Cortes would not tarry - he had an Aztec Empire to conquer - he was only the first conquistador to arrive in the region, and the Spanish established settlements on the coast and invaded the Yucatan in 1528 and again in 1535. It was only in 1542 that they were successful, and that was because the canny Xiu in Maní decided to leverage the Spanish presence by making an alliance. This pact with the devil did aid the Xiu in the short term, as they were able to

---

108   de Landa 1566 (1978). Pg 15-16
109   de Landa 1566 (1978). Pg 16
110   de Landa 1566 (1978). Pg 137

dominate local politics and re-create Mayan unity, but the last independent Yucatecan Dynasty fell in 1546.[111] Instead, the Maya were placed under the increasingly fanatical jurisdiction of the Bishop Diego de Landa, and in 1562, furious by what he saw as treasonous heresy from his own converts, de Landa collected all of the Maya books that he could get his hands on and burned them in the central plaza of Maní. He was quite successful by his standards, since only three known Mayan texts survived.

After the Spanish takeover, the Xiu were converted to Catholicism and abandoned their rituals at Uxmal, but perhaps not all of their subjects were so willing because the Spanish would occasionally report finding incense and offerings in the ruined temples late into the colonial period. Throughout that period, occasional Spanish tourists would visit Uxmal, enough that the city was never completely forgotten by non-Maya but not enough to excite international interest.

The outside world only sat up and took interest because of the remarkable work of two English-speaking scholars: Catherwood and Stevens. Their text, *Incidents of Travel in Central America, Chiapas & Yucatán* (1843), was an international sensation and fit into a growing interest in lost cities in the West.[112][113] However, the region was not available for research throughout much of the 19th century because the Mayan Revolt and the brutal Caste War set the region aflame.[114]

That situation eventually changed, and in 1893, an archaeological team working in Uxmal from Harvard created casts of a number of the most prominent buildings, including facades of the House of the Governor. These casts were dismantled and shipped to Chicago, where they were reconstructed for the famed Chicago Columbian Exhibition (also known as the World's Fair or the "White City"). These facades were visited by thousands of spectators, including a number of American architects, one of whom was the innovative Frank Lloyd Wright. Wright subsequently adopted many Puuc-style elements - even including Chaak masks - into a number of his buildings. This style, called the Maya Revival, reached its zenith upon the construction of the Charles Ennis House and the Aline Barnsdall House[115].

Since that point, Uxmal has been simultaneously an archaeological and touristic destination, in part due to its remarkable architecture but also because of its accessibility to visitors who come to the town of Merida. The Mexican government took a particular interest in its ancient heritage after the Mexican Revolution (which finished in 1920), and the ruins were declared patrimony of the state and given official protectors and interpreters. This status was further bolstered in 1996 after UNESCO recognized Uxmal as one of their World Heritage Sites, arguably the most prestigious award that can be given to an ancient site today.[116]

As a result, more than a millennium after it flourished, Uxmal is a remarkable mountain city that is

111   Martin and Grube (2000). Pgs 229-230
112   "John Lloyd Stephens and Frederick Catherwood: Exploring the Land of the Maya" by Nicoletta Maestri. Accessed online at: http://archaeology.about.com/od/mayaresearchers/a/Stephens-and-Catherwood.htm
113   "Frederick Catherwood's Lithographs" accessed online at: http://www.casa-catherwood.com/catherwoodinenglish.html
114   *The Caste War of the Yucatán* by Nelson A. Reed (2001). Stanford University Press. Pg 154.
115   Pohl (1999). Pg 107
116   ""Pre-Hispanic Town of Uxmal" at the UNESCO World Heritage List, accessed online at: http://whc.unesco.org/en/list/791

visited and studied by multitudes around the world, and it is still treasured in the hearts of Mayans and Mexicans in general. Furthermore, it continues to be gradually restored, with careful research leading to the rebuilding of important structures. Undoubtedly this continued work will give new insights in the coming years, and there is much still to learn about the beautiful and enigmatic ruins.

19th century illustrations depicting Uxmal

Timeline of Events in the Yucatan Postclassic Period

455 AD	Foundation of the first settlement at Chichén Itzá (est.)
750 AD	Foundation of the city of Uxmal (est.)
750 - 900 AD	Collapse of the Classic Maya states in the south
850 AD	Beginning of the Puuc Style (est.)
875-900 AD	The Reign of Lord Chaak in Uxmal
875-880 AD	Height of the Puuc Style in the Yucatán
925 AD	End of Royal Power in Uxmal End of the Classic Mayan Period
Mid 900s	Completion of the last stage of Pyramid of the Magician in Uxmal
Late 900s	Chichén is the dominant power in the Yucatan, Uxmal eclipsed
Early 1000s	Chichén is ruled by Toltec-influenced Leaders
1100s	First small settlements at Mayapán
1179	Fall of the Toltec city of Tula (est.)
Early 1200	Foundation of Maní by the Xiu (est.)
1221	Hunac Ceel's Vision
1222	Hunac Ceel's Conquest of Chichén Foundation of Mayapán as the Capital
1441	Fall of the Cocomes and the destruction of Mayapán, Uxmal begins final decline
1521	Cortes stops on the Mayan coast while traveling to Mexico
1528 & 1535	First and Second Spanish Invasion
1542	Spanish Conquest of Maní and the Xiu-Spanish Alliance
1546	Last Yucatecan cities fall to the Spanish
1562	The Great Auto-de-fé in Maní, destruction of the Mayan elite culture
1840s	Catherwood and Steven visit Uxmal and other cities The Maya led by the Cocomes and Itzaes rise up against Mexico
1890s	Harvard University Expedition studies site and brings casts to 1893 Chicago World's Fair, exciting international attention
1909	Sylvanus Morley mapped Uxmal
1975	Inauguration of nightly Lights and Sound exhibition
1996	Inscription of the site onto the UNESCO World Heritage List

Chichén Itzá and Mayapán

Chapter 1: Origins of Chichén Itzá

The precise origins of any great ancient city will probably be forever buried archaeologically under the weight of later construction and historically under the weight of later mythologizing. This is no doubt the case with Chichén Itzá, but while scholars may never be able to determine where and when the first ballgame was played at Chichén Itzá, they can piece together an understanding of why this particular city rose to prominence at the time it did.

The apogee of Mayan culture and influence was in the period known to Mesoamerican scholars as the "Classical" period. Ranging from to the 3rd-9th centuries, during this time the región was dominated by two great powers, Tikal and Calakmul, located far to the south of the Yucatán in the northern Highlands. To the west, central Mexico was dominated by the cities of Teotihuacan, Cholula and Monte Albán. This was a period of relative stability, though it probably didn't feel that way as the ruling dynasties of Tikal and Calakmul vied for power and fought numerous proxy wars through their many client states[117]. This period is comparable to the great "cold war" between Athens and Sparta in ancient Greece.

The name "Chichén Itzá" translates to "near the edge of the well of the Itzáes", which refers to at least one of the city's two cenotes. The cenotes certainly served as the primary reason for the city's placement, because sources of secure water are rare on the Peninsula and were thus greatly treasured by the locals. While the rainforest appears lush and water-filled, the porous nature of the bedrock means that stable sources of water are as precious here as they might be in a more overtly dry climate, and this also explains the enduring importance of the rain god Chaac for the Yucatecan Maya. Manuscripts date the settlement's founding at either 415-435 CE or 455 CE, but either way they appear to agree on the rough date of origin. This means that the city was founded at roughly the same time the Anglo-Saxons conquered Britain and Atilla was ravaging the European mainland. These dates fit well within the Classic period of Mayan history, but for centuries, the city was a small, little-known backwater[118].

The Classic period ended throughout Mesoamerica at roughly the same time, and it has been argued that this was due to climate changes. Certainly, the old polities were no longer able to hold onto power, and throughout Mesoamerica great empires crumbled and were replaced by numerous smaller states. Amongst the Maya, the collapse of this period affected the Highlands, so the center of Mayan culture moved north onto the limestone shelf of the Yucatán Peninsula, to cities like Mayapá, Uxmal, Tulum, Cobá and, most importantly, Chichén Itzá. This was also a period of great movements of people and ideas across Mesoamerica; while there have always been pan-Mesoamerican trends (such as the Ballgame), this period saw people moving at unprecedented rates. One of the eventual outcomes of this movement was the Toltec influence on Chichén Itzá (discussed further in depth in a later chapter), and more generally, it brought rapid growth to the cult of the feathered serpent, the god Kukulkan, who was called Quetzalcoatl amongst the Aztecs. This cult would eventually be centered on Chichén Itzá, and its importance was paralleled by the city's rise in stature.

---

117   *The Atlas of World Archaeology* by Paul G. Bahn (ed.) (2009). The Brown Reference Group Ltd. Pgs 170-171.
118   "Pre-Hispanic City of Chichen Itza" at the UNESCO World Heritage List, accessed online at:
       http://whc.unesco.org/en/list/483

El Castillo's base depicts Kukulkan on the west face of the northern stairway.

However, in its earliest days, Chichén Itzá was part of a larger subgroup of Mayan cities called the Puuc in the north of the Peninsula. The center of the distinctive Puuc architecture was the city of Uxmal, which was located to the west of Chichén Itzá. Puuc style was characterized by restrained, carefully ordered ornamentation. The buildings had smooth, stucco finishes and were often dominated by broad horizontal lines and building elements[119].

There are some elements of oral history that have survived amongst the Maya people describing the foundation of Chichén Itzá. The ruler of the city was known as the Itzá, but the word "Itzá" is actually a blurry one. While it appears in the city's name and the ruler's title, it is also used for the ethnic group that eventually dominated the city and survives in a remnant in northern Guatemala. Moreover, in oral legend the term also refers to the name of a caste of warriors from the nearby city of Mayapán (also a Puuc city) who rebelled against the Cocom (the title of Mayapán's priest-king) and fled Mayapán to found Chichén Itzá. It is possible that this caste then became an ethnicity over time and lent its name to both city and ruler. The legends also maintain that these Itzáes claimed descent from the god Kukulkan, but this was probably a later addition to the story, since the early city did not appear to be dedicated to Kukulkan but Chaac, the pan-Mayan rain god. The legend goes on to state that 120 years later, the Cocomes of Mayapán conquered Chichén Itzá, overthrew the Itzáes, and made the city a dependency of their state[120].

119   "Uxmal" in the *Encyclopedia Britannica*, accessed online at:
       http://www.britannica.com/EBchecked/topic/620988/Uxmal#ref225521
120   *The Myths of Mexico and Peru* by Lewis Spence. 1913 (2005). Barnes and Noble Books. Pg 133.

There is nothing implausible about these stories, though even if they are true, they only tell a portion of the story: the elite tale of war, rebellion and conquest. This tale does not explain why Chichén Itzá, amongst all of the tiny statelets that emerged in the chaos of the Postclassic Transformation, rose to become the mighty state and the Maya's most famous city. Archaeological evidence shows that as Cobá (the regional center in the Classic period) declined, Chichén Itzá and Uxmal (both in the west) rose up as allies or sister-cities to fill the gap. The Lord Chaak (ruler of Uxmal) expanded on land, while Chichén Itzá sought to capitalize on sea-going trade, and what the Itzáes brought to the trading table was salt, a vitally important and difficult-to-acquire nutrient. While today people think of salt as an everyday commodity, in the ancient world it was a rare and expensive commodity, hence the English expression "worth his weight in salt". Chichén Itzá controlled a coastal port named Isla Cerritos and one of the largest saltworks in Mesoamerica, called Emal[121].

During this period, the Itzáes built a ceremonial center in the core of the city that in many ways was typical of the surrounding Puuc centers. Today many of these buildings survive and make up the Southern Group of the ceremonial core. The most famous of these structures is the Caracol, an observatory similar to a building in Uxmal. The Caracol is decorated with images of the hook-nosed rain god Chaac, and all around it are other smaller buildings also done in a Puuc style, including the Red House, the Temple of the Lintels, and the House of the Deer[122]. They have the same austerity and dominant horizontal architectural elements as buildings in Uxmal, and furthermore, dates found on inscriptions of a set of buildings called the Nunnery Group in this complex date back to 875-880 CE, during the heyday of Uxmal[123] and before the 10th century rise of the cult of Kukulkan and the Toltec influence. Thus, these structures come from an era when Chichén Itzá would have been a young, up-and-coming power, allied to but probably still under the shadow of Uxmal.

---

121   "Chichén Itzá" in *Exploring Mesoamerica* by John M.D. Pohl (1999). Oxford University Press. Pgs 128-129.
122   "Chichén Itzá" in *Exploring Mesoamerica* by John M.D. Pohl (1999). Oxford University Press. Pgs 126-127.
123   Dated as the reign of Lord Chaak: 875-890 CE.

Picture of the Red House taken by Régis Lachaume

As a result, by combining the archaeological record and oral history, scholars can piece together a probable origin for Chichén Itzá. A group of warrior rebels called the Itzá from Mayapán (or perhaps another city lost to time) fled their city and either founded or conquered a small settlement near the coast which they named for themselves. In the chaos of the early Post-Classic, they allied themselves with an older dynasty in the neighboring city of Uxmal and their famous king Lord Chaak, after which they started emulating the Uxmal elites' Puuc architectural style. The Itzáes specialized in seaborne trade and salt mining, carving out an increasingly lucrative niche for themselves, and though they may have been conquered temporarily by their former overlords, this does not halt their growing commercial success or their connections with exotic societies across the Gulf of Mexico. In fact, it is foreign influence, primarily from the Toltecs of Central Mexico, that would forever reshape the city.

As the Postclassic period began in earnest, the neighboring city of Uxmal began to decline. By 925 CE, all of the central buildings of this other city were abandoned, along with most of the other Puuc centers. Uxmal was not forgotten - the powerful Xiu family would view it as their place of origin and venerate its shrines until the Spanish Conquest - but it was forever eclipsed. Mayapán would continue under the Cocomes until the Spanish Conquest, though it also did not ascend again in the Postclassic period. By the late 900s, the only power left in the region was Chichén Itzá[124].

---

124   "Uxmal" in *Exploring Mesoamerica* by John M.D. Pohl (1999). Oxford University Press. Pgs 106-117.

While Chichén Itzá began its rise by controlling the local trade in salt, it began to diversify as it was drawn into a trade network dominated at the time by its eventual sister-city Tula, the capital of the Toltec peoples. The Toltec are one of the most famous Mesoamerican groups, but they are also the most controversial and mysterious. The Toltec have been identified as the group that established a strong state centered in Tula, and the Aztec claimed the Toltec as their cultural predecessors, so much so that the word Toltec comes from the Aztec's word Tōltēcatl, translated as artisan. The Aztec also kept track of the Toltec's history, including keeping a list of important rulers and events, that suggest the peak of the Toltec occurred from about 900-1100 CE

However, unlike the Mayans, the Aztecs are not widely viewed or remembered with nuance, in part because their own leader burned extant Aztec writings and rewrote a mythologized history explaining his empire's dominance less than a century before the Spanish arrived. Thus, even as historians have had to rely on Aztec accounts to trace the history and culture of the Toltec, they have had to deal with the fact that the evidence is fragmentary and incomplete. Given the fact that the Aztec leaders engaged in revisionist history, it becomes even more difficult to be sure that the Aztec accounts of the Toltec are accurate, with some scholars going so far as to call the Toltec culture nothing but myth.

While scholars continue to debate whether the Toltec were an actual historical group, there is an added layer of mystery to the fact that the settlement at Tula has a lot in common with Chichén Itzá. The architecture and art at both sites are so similar that archaeologists and anthropologists have assumed they had the same cultural influences, even as historians struggle to determine the historical timelines, and thus whether Tula influenced Chichén Itzá or vice versa.

The Toltecs were masters at long-distance trade, and they controlled numerous sea routes across the Gulf of Mexico, bringing obsidian and turquoise down from the deserts of what is today northern Mexico and the U.S. Southwest.[125] Meanwhile, from the southern region of what is today Guatemala and Nicaragua, the Itzáes brought up gold and cacao, and they began to grow cotton locally. Evidence of the great extent of this network has been found in Pueblo Bonito, a 9th-12th century settlement in Chaco Canyon in the northwestern corner of today's New Mexico. A major site inhabited by the ancestors of today's Puebloan peoples, it was the final terminus of trade routes that began far to the south of Chichén Itzá. The locals mined turquoise and tanned buffalo hides for trade, and one of the most important items they bought were massive quantities of vivid red macaw feathers carried up from Central America. At least some if not the great majority of these feathers would have passed through the markets of Chichén Itzá and the city's port on their journey north[126].

During this period, Chichén Itzá was probably viewed by its neighbors as a cosmopolitan center, a place where one might encounter people from strange cities across the seas, from the legendary deserts of the far north, from the fallen mountain kingdoms of the southern Maya, or the strange jungles of the deep south. With the possible exception of the great Toltec city of Tula to the north, there was, for the Mesoamericans, no place on Earth quite like Chichén Itzá.

---

125   A form of black volcanic glass that is perhaps the finest quality stone for the making of stone tools, but is only found in a handful of locations in Mesoamerica.
126   "Mesoamerican Themes and Chaco Canyon" by F.J. Mathien (1997). Accessed online at: http://www.colorado.edu/Conferences/chaco/mesomod.htm

Precious stones were not the only import from central Mexico. As the other Puuc cities declined or disappeared around Chichén Itzá, the future metropolis began to track its own unique course. Somewhere in the 9th century, the city's rulers began to consciously, actively, and at great cost import a series of cultural, religious, political and architectural innovations from their trading partners in Tula. Perhaps the most important import of this period was the worship of the god Kukulkan. The name "Kukulkan" means the "Feathered Serpent," the same meaning of his Toltec name "Quetzalcoatl." He was associated with jade stones, the creator of humanity (through the sacrifice of his own blood), and the giver of maize to his creations. He was said to have been tricked into committing incest with his sister and set himself on fire out of remorse after he learned the truth. He then rose to heaven and became Venus, which as already noted was extremely important to the early Itzáes who built the Caracol. Other legends held that he crossed the sea on a boat, promising to return in the future[127], the very legend Hernan Cortes would utilize to his advantage when conquering the Aztec.

The ancient Mesoamericans had a worldview which was relatively flexible when it came to the addition of gods and other supernatural beings to their pantheons. Even Christianity was absorbed by the Maya as yet another divinity, and today Yucatec shamans are comfortable extorting the rain god Chaac in one breath and the Virgin Mary in the next. Thus, Kukulkan was probably worshiped alongside other deities on the Peninsula without too much anxiety, and it was probably inevitable that the cult of the Feathered Serpent would enter the Mayan region through the port city of Chichén Itzá.

However, what is surprising is that it the Itzáes appear to have wholeheartedly accepted Kukulkan as their deity and made their city the center of his worship throughout the Mayan lands. This is most evident in the construction of El Castillo, which apparently served as the Temple of Kukulkan in the new, Toltec-influenced northern section of the urban core. Unquestionably one of the most impressive monuments in ancient Mesoamerica, El Castillo is a square structure that runs 60 meters (190 feet) on each side and reaches a height of 12 meters (40 feet). It is built in a step-style, like the Mesopotamian ziggurats or early Egyptian pyramids, but not like the smooth surfaces of later Egyptian pyramids, such as those at Giza. At the center of each of the four sides is a broad staircase, and modern climbers quickly discover the remarkable steepness of the staircase and the narrowness of the stairs themselves, which require the climber to often turn his or her feet sideways for a good footing and sometimes to lean forward, scrambling on not just feet but also hands. This was probably intended, as it would cause the devotee to clamber up in a semi-prostrate position before the might of Kukulkan.

El Castillo is also much broader than the typical Mayan pyramids, giving it a squat profile that is reminiscent of pyramids found around Central Mexico in places like Cholula, Tula, Teotihuacan and Tenochtitlan. The Maya often built their pyramids in stages, by sheathing a preexisting pyramid in a new layer of stone, burying the old one, and thereby creating a taller, broader replacement. Excavations by the Mexican government in the 20th century found two smaller pyramids subsumed within the current exterior. These older pyramids appeared to blend the Mayan and Toltec influences more than the last incarnation, which does away with the hybrid styles and predominantly favors the

127   "Kukulkan" and "Quetzalcoatl" at the *Encyclopedia Mythica*. Accessed online at: http://www.pantheon.org/. "Kukulcan" at the *Mythology Dictionary*. Accessed online at: http://www.mythologydictionary.com/kukulcan-mythology.html

Toltec elements.[128]

The north side of El Castillo

El Castillo was only one of a large number of Toltec-influenced buildings[129]. Near the Castillo is the Tzompantli, a low platform decorated with images of jaguars and eagles. It has no antecedents in Mayan architecture, but it's remarkably similar to the Tzompantli in Central Mexico, which held wood scaffolds that were used to display the decapitated heads of opponents. Chichén Itzá also has a Temple of the Warriors, famous for its elaborate colonnades and still covered in carvings of dramatic Toltec-style warriors[130].

---

128   "Chichen Itza" in *Exploring Mesoamerica* by John M.D. Pohl (1999). Oxford University Press. Pgs 121
129   "Chichen Itza and the Toltec Question" in *The Chronicle of the Mayan Kings and Queens: Deciphering the Dynasties of the Ancient Maya* by Simon Martin and Nikolai Grube (2000). Thames and Hudson. Pg 229.
130   "Chichen Itza" in *Exploring Mesoamerica* by John M.D. Pohl (1999). Oxford University Press. Pgs 122-124

The Temple of the Warriors. Photo by Keith Pomakis

The Temple of the Warriors' columns

Statue of Chaac Mool located at the Temple of the Warriors. Photo by Bjørn Christian Tørrissen.

However, perhaps the most striking difference for the Maya themselves cannot be easily seen architecturally. Chichén Itzá had no King, despite the fact kingship was the definitive element of the Classic Mayan polity. The relationship between the king and the gods on the one hand and the king and his subjects on the other lay at the heart of Mayan politics; the king was seen to make sacrifices - often of his own blood - in order to please the gods and continue to bring their blessings down on the city. When the king failed in his duties and the gods were displeased, their boons - like regular rainfall - were withdrawn. The kings were also considered to be the high priests of the patron gods of the cities. Much of Mayan art, history and architecture is focused upon the personage of the king and his family, their ancestors and their glorious deeds.

Conversely, the Toltec leaders of Tula did not inherit their power through their family genealogy. Instead, they were elected by other elites (the heads of important families) and confirmed by the high priests of the two most important gods, one of which was Quetzalcoatl/Kukulkan. It appears that the government of Chichén Itzá was similarly organized, because there are no references to the dynastic origins of leaders and many inscriptions are puzzlingly free of reference to a king altogether, something unheard of at earlier Mayan sites. There are also no references to leaders as "brothers" or "companions." This has led scholars to theorize that Chichén Itzá may have been a confederacy of powerful families dedicated to the worship of Kukulkan. Perhaps this institution, which was obviously inspired by that of the Toltecs, emerged from the early Itzá warrior brotherhood, or it may have been made up of local elites from other towns like the Xius of Uxmal and Cocomes of Mayapán. Regardless of its origin, it is yet another example of the broad differences between Chichén Itzá and the traditional Mayan polity[131].

Chapter 2: The Era of Chichén Itzá's Glory

According to oral histories collected amongst the Yucatecan Maya in the modern period, Chichén Itzá began to peak when its leaders joined up with the Xiu family (the former leaders of Uxmal) to overthrow the Cocomes of Mayapán. Uxmal had been obliterated by Mayapán during a previous war, but now its rulers exacted vengeance. This history is a bit jumbled because the date given for these events is 1436 CE, long after the archaelogical record shows Chichén Itzá had risen and fallen,[132] but it is still possible that the general outline of events is correct. If Uxmal/Xiu and Chichén Itzá were allies against Mayapán and the Cocomes for dominance of the northern Yucatán, the fighting may represent a breakdown of an earlier confederation[133]. This may also be proof that Chichén Itzá was at one point merely an outpost of Toltec culture in the south or as a center for transcontinental trade before becoming a Mayan superpower.

Eventually, however, Chichén Itzá rose to prominence and began to exert influence influence on other Mayan city-states and the ways of life of both elites and commoners during its heyday. The easiest indication of the spread of Chichén Itzá's influence is the expansion of the cult of Kukulkan throughout the Mayan region. Evidence suggests that the surrounding cities adopted the worship of Kukulkan wholeheartedly; for example, temples were erected in Mayapán and the Spanish documented a grand yearly festival dedicated to the god in the center of Maní, which was run by the Xiu family. Other Postclassic Yucatán cities also developed temples to the god, and even the little walled city of Tulum on the eastern shore had a Temple to the Wind God[134]. In the Highlands, the Qui'che Maya incorporated the "Sovereign Plumed Serpent" into the heart of their mythology as the creator of the world, as written in a sacred book called the *Popol Vuh*. Its opening passage reads in part:

> "Whatever there is that might be is simply not there: only the pooled water, only the calm sea, only it alone is pooled. Whatever might be is simply not there: only murmurs, ripples in the dark, in the night. Only the Maker, Modeler alone, Sovereign Plumed Serpent, the Bearers, Begetters are in the water, a glittering light. They are there, they are enclosed in quetzal feathers, in blue-green. Thus the name,

---

131   "Chichen Itza" in *Exploring Mesoamerica* by John M.D. Pohl (1999). Oxford University Press. Pg 129
132   *The Myths of Mexico and Peru* by Lewis Spence. 1913 (2005). Barnes and Noble Books. Pg 135.
133   However, some archaeologists have dated Mayapán as a later city, after the decline of both of its neighbors - the debate is still out.
134   "Zona Arqueológica de Tulum" at the National Institute of Anthropology and History of Mexico Homepage http://www.inah.gob.mx/index.php?option=com_content&view=article&id=5491

'Plumed Serpent.' They are great knowers, great thinkers in their very being.[135]

Perhaps the most telling evidence of the god's eventual importance comes from the Lacandon Maya, the last non-Christianized Mayan group. The Lacandon Maya continue to practice their ancient religion in their small isolated homesteads deep in the Lacandon jungle on the opposite side of the Highlands from Chichén Itzá. These tiny farms are perhaps the most distant spot of the Mayan world from the great pyramid of Kukulkan (El Castillo), yet even here Kukulkan makes an appearance as the flying serpent companion of the sun god[136].

So what was life like in the shadow of the splendor of the Pyramid of Kukulkan? For the elites, it probably seemed to be the center of the universe. Within sight of the pyramid, archaeologists have found a grand market where goods came and went, including local salt, cotton, precious stones, worked copper, gold, tools, cacao, feathers, and furs. The elite no doubt took advantage of this abundant wealth and garbed themselves and their homes in the finest things available. Their homes had large areas for entertaining and were decorated with elaborate frescoes[137], and the Mayan leadership was infamous for their grand parties, including competitive drinking, feasting, and numerous forms of performative art such as dancing, music, jesting, storytelling and theater.

Even more important than mercantile pursuits were the ritual duties. In addition to the Pyramid, there were numerous other temples around the Core, and the elite was expected to participate in elaborate rituals, including bloodletting from early childhood. All Maya gave of their own blood to the gods, but the leaders were held to a higher standard of sacrifice, and this would have been all the more important in Chichén Itzá because the city was undoubtedly a center for pilgrimage. The rest of the Mayan world looked to the leaders of Chichén Itzá to hold up the standard for appropriate worship of Kukulkan. Thus, moreso than in other cities, the Chichén elite were under even more pressure to perform their ritual duties, not just from their own people but also from foreign observers as well[138].

Given its prestige and the importance of rituals, it is perhaps not surprising that seemingly everyone in the city participated in much of the ritual life. El Castillo appears to have been designed with a broad courtyard at its base so that crowds of spectators could watch, and every kind of inhabitant would have benefited from the presence of a diverse marketplace. Moreover, many were probably proud of their citizenship in what seemed to be the world's mightiest city, and there was no better place to be devoted to the worship of the "Sovereign Plumed Serpent."

That said, the lives of the commoners, who comprised the vast majority of the population even in a wealthy city-state like Chichén Itzá, were not nearly as glamorous as those of the leadership. While the archaeology for this group is not as well developed as those of the elite, a lot can be gleaned from the

135   *Popol Vuh: The Definitive Edition of the Mayan Book of the Dawn of Life and the Glories of Gods and Kings*. Dennis Tedlock (Trans.) (1996). Touchstone Books. Quote on pg 64
136   *Handbook of Mesoamerican Mythology* by Kay Almere Read and Jason González (2000). Oxford University Press. Pg 201
137   This is an art form with considerable antiquity amongst the Maya; perhaps the most important surviving frescoes are in the ruins of Bonampak.
138   "The Royal Culture of the Maya" in *The Chronicle of the Mayan Kings and Queens: Deciphering the Dynasties of the Ancient Maya* by Simon Martin and Nikolai Grube (2000). Thames and Hudson. Pgs 14-16.

accounts of early Spanish observers. Diego de Landa, the infamous Spanish bishop who burned Maya texts, wrote an elaborate description of the Yucatán to people back home. He described the peasantry as living in wooden homes with whitewashed walls and steeply-pitched thatched roofs. He noted that near their homes, they maintained fields of their own as well as commonly-farmed fields that were controlled by local elites, growing primarily corn (maize) but also cacao, chili peppers and vegetables. In the forests and swamps, they hunted venison, manatees, fish and wild fowl.[139]

De Landa described the traditional male attire, which has been confirmed by comparing it to images in frescoes and books, as "a strip of cloth a hand broad that served for breeches and leggings, and which they wrapped several times about the waist, leaving one end hanging in front and one behind. These ends were embroidered by their wives with much care and with featherwork. They wore large square mantles, which they threw over the shoulders. They wore sandals of hemp or deerskin tanned dry, and then no other garments." The women wore skirts and, in some regions, covered their torsos with doubled-sided mantles they fastened below the armpits. But for others, "their sole garment is a long wide sack, open at the sides, reaching to the thighs and there fastened by its own ends." Even today, the Mayan women are renowned for their embroidery. According to De Landa, Mayan women also had elaborate hairdos, including "coiffures as fine as those of the most coquettish Spanish women", and they decorated themselves with piercings, tattoos, body paint and by filing their teeth. Of course, all of these clothes and decorations were finer and more elaborate amongst the elites than the poor.[140]

As these descriptions make clear, at the height of Chichén Itzá's power, the society there was centralized, highly-organized and strictly stratified between social classes. For those who controlled it, Chichén Itzá's wealth allowed for incredible displays of power and sophistication. Indeed, the city's leadership developed a standard for ritual and elegance that set the standard for the entire Mayan region and served to promote not only their trading influence but also the cult of Kukulkan. For those at the bottom, life in Chichén Itzá was much like the peasant life elsewhere, consisting of long, labor-filled hours on personal and elite-owned plots of land, with small homes and rich family life.

---

139   *Yucatan Before and After the Conquest* by Friar Diego de Landa. William Gates (trans.) 1566 (1978). Dover Books. Pgs 32-39, 93-101
140   *Yucatan Before and After the Conquest* by Friar Diego de Landa. William Gates (trans.) 1566 (1978). Dover Books. Pgs 33, 53-54

Chapter 3: Description of the Site of Chichen Itzá

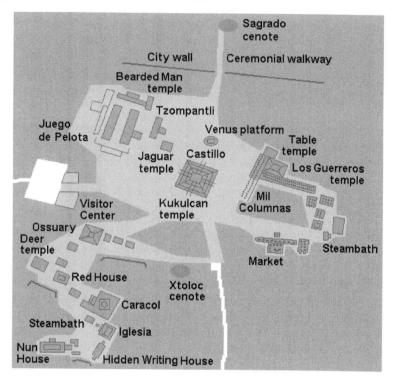

The layout at Chichén Itzá

Every year, on the days of the Autumnal and Vernal Equinox, crowds gather at the base of the Castillo, the spectacular stepped pyramid at the heart of the Mayan city of Chichén Itzá. Slowly, over the course of the day, the shadows cast by the pyramid's corners seems to slither down the balustrade of the principal stairway. This ancient site, whose construction was perhaps performed around the same time of the first great Gothic cathedrals of Europe, was dedicated to the serpent god Kukulkan, a connection which seems to give meaning to the twice-a-year appearance of the snake[141].

141   "The Sunlight Effect of the Kukulcán Pyramid or The History of a Line" by Tomás García-Salgado. In the *Nexus Network Journal*. Accessed online at: http://perspectivegeometry.com/sitebuildercontent/sitebuilderfiles/kululcanpg.pdf on 1 Oct 2013.

Photo of the serpent effect at El Castillo during the spring equinox in 2009

The serpent effect at night using artificial light. Photo by Bjørn Christian Tørrissen.

While El Castillo is the most distinctive building on the site, Chichén Itzá was far more than simply a ceremonial center. In fact, it was one of the most visually spectacular and important cities economically, politically and culturally during the period of Mayan history known as the Postclassic, making it arguably the mightiest city ever built among the Mayans, and dwarfing the earlier regional "superpowers" of Tikal and Calakmul.

The city's size and obvious power has attracted archaeological attention for decades, and that work is ongoing as more of the site is excavated, but Chichén Itzá is also unique among other sites in Mesoamerica for the way it fused Mayan art and architecture with styles coming from the Toltec peoples around the area north of what is today Mexico City. While early archaeologists theorized that Chichén Itzá might have been an eastern capital of an empire originating in the Toltec capital of Tula (the equivalent of considering Chichén to be the Byzantium to Tula's Rome), these theories have found little support in the archaeological record. Today, scholars tend to believe that the Toltec influence was based on trade and religious links. Regardless of the source, this Toltec influence fused with earlier Puuc Mayan forms to create unique art and a cosmopolitan city where goods, ideas and people from across Mesoamerica met.

The Tzompantli ("Skull Platform") at Chichén Itzá displays skulls impaled vertically on the wall, a style influenced by the Toltec. Photo by Bjørn Christian Tørrissen.

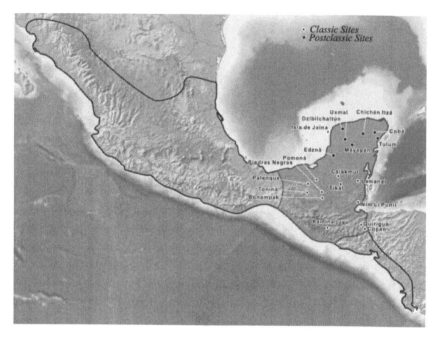

Map of the Mayan Empire

The Mayan world is divided amongst the Lowlands of the Yucatán peninsula (Mexico's answer to Florida, jutting into the Gulf of Mexico) and the Highlands of today's Guatemala, and the Mexican state of Chiapas. Chichén Itzá is firmly located in the Lowlands, close to the northern Gulf shore. Unlike Florida, which is in essence a glorified sand bar, the Yucatán is set on firm bedrock: a broad shelf of limestone and similar rocks called the Yucatán Shelf. Covering the Peninsula is a thick tropical rainforest that is home to species like the tapir, jaguar, toucan, and scarlet macaws. This geology means that there are almost no topographically distinguishing marks on the landscape, so the pyramids of the ancient cities and the church spires of the new ones are the only break to the endless green monotony. Driving west from the modern tourist city of Cancún to the ruins of Chichén Itzá, visitors cross a very flat landscape on arrow-straight roads that seem to run through an endless canyon of jungle green.

The geography of this landscape defines much of what was (and still is) possible agriculturally and socially. Rainforests concentrate nutrients in the bodies of trees, leaving the soils relatively thin and por, meaning the Mayans who lived in the area could benefit from the normal rainforest agricultural technique of swidden.[142] To understand better the techniques of the ancient residents of Chichén Itzá,

---

142   Swidden agriculture, previously called "slash-and-burn" agriculture involves the cutting and burning of a small area of the rainforest and then using the ashes as fertilizer for several seasons of crops. However, fertility gained by this

one need look no further tan the contemporary Mayan community of Cobá, living to the south and west of the ruins[143]. The residents of Cobá live densely packed into a small central town much smaller than Chichén Itzá, with small outlying settlements of a handful of buildings in the forest. The community of Cobá owns the surrounding forest communally, and a farmer's council divides up land into *milpas*, fields which the individual then clears. Once cleared, the farmer searches the thin soil for places where the subsoil limestone is worn away into a soil-filled hole and then plants corn and other crops into these holes, with different crops needing holes of differing depths. This gives the *milpa* a disorganized appearance, with crops scattered apparently randomly across its area.

Archaeologist Ellen Kintz, who studied these contemporary Maya, has argued that the ancient Yucatecan cities like Chichén Itzá would have functioned in much the same way, only on a much wider scale. As the crops could never be planted densely, they had a need for a wide area to support the urban core, a reality which added to the Mayan system of scattered independent city-states.[144] Mayan farms produced a variety of crops, the staples being corn or maize with beans and squashes. In some Maya communities, cotton, cocoa and honey were produced, and whatever wasn't used for basic living was traded. Along the coast of modern Belize, Maya agricultural practices included the use of irrigation ditches, mounded fields and reclamation of swamp land. These techniques would have ensured a very long period of productivity for agriculture.

Just as modern Mexico has found it easy to construct straight highways across the jungle, so too did the ancient Maya. In fact, many of their highways, which were elevated above the surface of the jungle floor on a terrace-like structure, still exist today. They fanned out from Chichén Itzá and her sister cities, not only connecting the different city-states but also serving to connect the agricultural outlands with the core settlements. These roads allowed farmers to walk to and from their fields every day, since the Pre-Columbian Mesoamericans had no domesticated pack animals.

The urban core of Chichén Itzá was, at its height, roughly 15 square miles (or 25 square kilometers), making it roughly half the size of the New York City borough of Staten Island. Most of this ruin remains covered with rainforest today, so only the core structures - roughly analogous to the National Mall in Washington D.C. - has been cleared and restored. These outer areas would have been characterized by buildings in the pole and thatch style: a framework of poles set into the ground, with walls made of branches between them which gave privacy but also allowed for breezes to enter. The roofs were thatched with local grasses. However, in increasingly wealthier districts of the city, there is a greater percentage of stone buildings, which had the distinct advantage of being relatively impervious to the hurricanes that too often sweep across the region.

---

way is quickly used up and the swidden farmer must then move on to other sites - often moving his or her entire settlement to uncut territories. The Mayans would never have been able to build stable, long-term cities if they used up the soil in this way in the span of a few years.

143   Though we must always take care while making such comparisons, as obviously much has changed in the centuries since the fall of Chichén Itzá and the present day - perhaps most significantly the destruction of the Mayan religio-political system and its replacement by first Spanish and then Mexican dominance of the region. However, today's Maya do work under the same geographical and climatological constraints and so some careful comparisons can be made.

144   *Life Under the Tropical Canopy: Tradition and Change Among the Yucatec Maya* by Ellen Kintz (1990). Case Studies in Cultural Anthropology.

The buildings were arranged into compounds, which were probably associated with extended families. Compounds included a number of buildings, one of which was a kitchen (removed from the others to protect against the threat of fire), and an open area that probably had small vegetable gardens and tres for fruits, nuts, and fuel. However, unfortunately little is known about the lives of these "suburbanites" and their neighborhoods, as almost all archaeological attention at the site has been focused on the spectacular ceremonial core.

When the Yucatán is blessed with rainfall, the porous nature of the underlying limestone (the same porousness that allows for the *milpa* style of cultivation) means that almost all of the water is absorbed into the bedrock, so the Peninsula has almost no surface water sources, whether lakes or rivers. This was true of Chichén Itzá, which is not located on a river or lake. Instead, the citizens drew their water primarily from two great open sinkholes called *cenotes*. *Cenotes* were considered to be sacred, so sacred that one of the cenotes at Chichén Itzá was used only for ritual purposes and is today called the Sacred Cenote. The Sacred Cenote is located to the north of the city center and was connected to it by a ritual causeway. Residents offered precious goods here to the rain god Chaac, who is still sometimes invoked by nearby residents, in hopes of rain and good harvest[145]. The other water source, Cenote Xlacah, probably served as the primary well for the citizenry[146].

Photo of the Sacred Cenote by Emil Kehnel

All Mayan cities had a ceremonial core, the district of grand stone buildings and broad courtyards at the heart of the city that served as the religious, political, military and probably economic focal point of the city. This district was also the organizing nexus for the entire city-state and the place where the governing elite demonstrated their wealth and power in works of art and elaborate ritual. The ceremonial core of Chichén Itzá was located a few hundred yards to the south of the Sacred Cenote,

145   "A Tour of Chichen Itza with a Brief History of the Site and its Archaeology" by Jorge Peréz de Lara. Accessed online at: http://www.mesoweb.com/chichen/features/tour/index.html on 1 Oct 2013
146   "Archaeological Survey at Chichen Itza" by George F. Andrews of the University of Oregon. Accessed online at: repositories.lib.utexas.edu. Pg 3.

and it has been divided by historians into two parts: an older section to the south consisting of styles similar to the Puuc Maya tradition of surrounding cities and a younger, grander section to the north which emulates styles from the Toltec city of Tula far to the west.

Dominating the north is the spectacular symmetrical pyramid El Castillo, which is actually only the outermost layer of a pyramid that was expanded several times over the city's long history.[147] Meanwhile, other principal buildings of ancient Chichén Itzá included the Tzompantli (or Skull Platform), the Temple of Jaguars, the Temple of Warriors, the Caracol and the Nunnery. It is immediately apparent that most of these names were applied by the Spanish Conquistadores (such as El Castillo) or English-speaking archaeologists who created names based on physical description (such as the "Red House" near the Caracol) or by guessing its function (like "The High Priests' Temple" at the north end of the southern group).

The High Priests' Temple

The Caracol[148] is almost as famous as El Castillo itself, and it has also attracted interest for decades. The name is Spanish for "snail," a term that comes from a spiral staircase within the structure's central turret, which looks something like a snail-shell when looked at from above. Like many Mayan buildings, the Caracol was constructed on a broad stone platform, and the structure rises above its neighbors, dominating the southern complex of buildings. The most prominent feature of the Caracol is the circular tower at the top of it. While much of the tower has fallen over the centuries, the remaining walls have windows which appear to have functioned as siting guides for ancient observers tracking the Sun and the planet Venus, crucially important celestial features for the Maya. A document called the Dresden Codex from roughly the same time period as Chichén Itzá's glory days describes Venus as

147   "Chichén Itzá" in *Exploring Mesoamerica* by John M.D. Pohl (1999). Oxford University Press. Pgs 118-131.
148   This should not be confused a Mayan site in modern-day Belize that is today known as "Caracol," a site of considerable importance which was larger than Belize City and held a population greater than Belize itself.

Chak Ek', or "The Great Star." It appears to have been seen as the harbinger of war, death and victory. Battles between the mightiest cities (of which Chichén Itzá was certainly one) were described as "Star Wars," certainly a reference to Chake Ek' and other stars whose motions may have been carefully tracked at the Caracol.[149] The Grolier Codex, which was written around 1230 CE, and the Dresden Codex, written just before the Spanish conquest, have tables for the plotting of the phases of Venus, Mars, and solar eclipses.

Photo of the Caracol by Daniel Schwen

---

149   "Venus: The War Star" in *The Chronicle of the Mayan Kings and Queens: Deciphering the Dynasties of the Ancient Maya* by Simon Martin and Nikolai Grube (2000). Thames and Hudson. Pg 16. "El Caracol: A Maya Observatory" at the Virginia University Astronomy Department, accessed online at: http://www.astro.virginia.edu/class/oconnell/astr121/el-caracol.html

Photo of the observatory by Bruno Girin

Another important feature of the center was the Grand Ballcourt. The Mesoamerican ballgame was a combination of sporting event and religious ritual that was practiced not only throughout the Mayan region but up through what became the Aztec Empire, spreading from modern-day Nicaragua even all the way north to modern-day Arizona. In most Maya cities that have been excavated, there is at least one ball court, indicating the central importance of the game now referred to as pok-ta-pok. The long rectangular structures with sloping or vertical walls along the sides were the sites of a game in which two teams of 2-7 people moved a rubber ball by hitting it with the body without the use of hands or feet. The most effective method of directing the ball was through the use of the hips. The goal was to pass the ball through a vertical circular ring attached to the long wall of the court.

This game or a variant of it was important in several Mesoamerican cultures, but based on the archeological evidence the Maya considered it to be a central feature in their urban life. The game played such a central role in courtly life that one of the common titles for a Mayan king was "aj pItzál" ("ballplayer").[150] Moreover, sculptures associated with ball courts suggest that the game concluded with ritual human sacrifice, presumably captives, although some have suggested that the losing team or the captain of the team were treated to sacrificial execution. This procedure makes sense in the light of the theory that the game was a way of settling municipal grievances or inter-city wars. If the game was merely played for the sake of entertainment and competition, a ritual sacrifice of the losers would have been a rather severe method of improving the quality of play.

The stone ring at the Grand Ballcourt in Chichén Itzá was nearly 30 feet off the ground. Photo by Kåre Thor Olsen.

At Chichén Itzá, archaeologists have found the largest known Ballcourt in the world. Shaped like a capital "I," it was 140 meters (470 feet long) with a width of 35 meters (115 feet). The walls around it, where the hoops were located, are 10 meters high (32 feet). Around these walls are six sets of stone panels, carved with bas relief images of ballplayers girded in armor resembling something between a modern American football player and a full-out Mayan warrior[151]. Nowhere else have archaeologists found such a vast playing ground, leading many to surmise that the "game" was more pageant than sport here. Undoubtedly, it was seen by the city's elites as crucially important to their power structure, or they otherwise would have never invested such energy in its infrastructure.

150   "The Royal Culture of the Maya" in *The Chronicle of the Mayan Kings and Queens: Deciphering the Dynasties of the Ancient Maya* by Simon Martin and Nikolai Grube (2000). Thames and Hudson. Pg 15
151   "Chichén Itzá" in *Exploring Mesoamerica* by John M.D. Pohl (1999). Oxford University Press. Pgs 123-124.

Photo of the Grand Ballcourt taken from El Castillo. Photo by André Möller

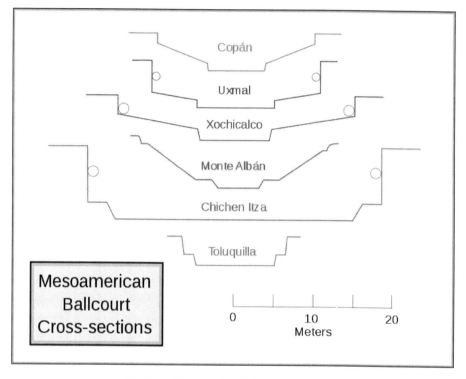

Copán

Uxmal

Xochicalco

Monte Albán

Chichen Itza

Toluquilla

Mesoamerican Ballcourt Cross-sections

0   10   20
        Meters

The size of different Mesoamerican ballcourts based on locations

Chapter 4: The Decline of Chichén Itzá and the Rise of Mayapán

Unlike the Mesoamerican cities conquered by the Spanish, like the Incan city of Cuzco and the Aztec city of Tenochtitlan, the fall of Chichén Itzá was not documented in any surviving books. It seems the city was not conquered and therefore did not collapse in fire and blood. Instead, it apparently faded away over time and became abandoned, and since this process occurred gradually over an extended period of time, the causes of Chichén Itzá's collapse are likely complex and shifting. It also means historians may never be able to determine all of the root causes or understand just how Chichén Itzá met its end.

However, it's important not to confuse complexity and obscurity with "mystery." Much has been made in some documentaries and popular writing about "mysterious" places of the ancient past like Chichén Itzá, Stonehenge or the Moai of Easter Island, a process that opens the doors for wild theories, such as those that claim El Castillo was dedicated to ancient alien astronauts. While the details of how Chichén Itzá was first founded and how it declined are difficult archaeological questions, there is nothing that scholars have encountered in the archaeological record that cannot be understood without relying on extraterrestrial or supernatural explanations. The buildings of Chichén Itzá are impressive by any standard, but they're all the more impressive because archaeologists can understand the techniques used by their ancient human builders, and how these designs evolved out of earlier ones. Likewise, elements of the city's decline are still unknown, but there is nothing to suggest abnormal factors were involved. Cities across the world have declined naturally for a variety of reasons, like climate change, military conquest, shifting trade routes, exhausted natural resources, declining harvests, drought, or pestilence. Furthermore, the notion that the Maya were "lost" or disappeared is an absurd one because many Maya still live in the región; in fact, they make up the majority of the population of Guatemala and are considerable minorities in Belize and the Mexican states of Quintana Roo, Yucatán, Campeche, Chiapas and the nation of Belize.

For their part, the Maya themselves tell a tale regarding the proximate cause for Chichén Itzá's decline, the story of Canek:

> "A king of Chichén called Canek fell desperately in love iwth a young princess, who, whether she did not return his affection or whether she was compleled ot obey a parental mandate, married a more powerful Yucatec *cacique*. The discarded lover, unable to bear his loss, and moved by love and despair, armed his dependents and suddenly fell upon his successful rival. Then the gaiety of the feast was exchanged for the din of war, and amidst the confusion, the u Chichén prince disappeared, carrying off the beautiful bride. But conscious that his power was less than his rival's, and fearing his vengeance, he fled the country with most of his vassals."[152]

Of course, this story does not explain the disappearance of what was at one point the mightiest city in the region. For one, it claims that the "king" who ruled Chichén Itzá had more powerful enemies, so if that was true, the city was already in decline. It appears probable, however, that there is some kernel of truth here, because it is known that at one point, as the city began to fade, a group of Itzáes fled not only the city but the Lowlands in general. These refugees arrived in an area of modern-day Guatemala and settled on the lake now known as Petén Itzá, Guatemala's second-largest lake[153]. By the time the Spanish arrived to the región, the Itzáes still ruled the area from the city of Tayasal[154]. Tayasal was not one of the great Mayan capitals, but it is distinctive for a number of reasons, not the least of which is that it was the last independent Mayan city-state to be conquered by the Spanish. It was built upon an island and was well-fortified and isolated. If Canek and his followers truly built a fortress to protect themselves from the wrath of their enemies, they were at least successful in creating a bastion that outlasted every other.

Today, the last remnant of the Itzá' branch of the Mayan language can be found amongst a handful of elderly speakers in the Highlands of Guatemala near Lake Petén Itzá. While this is far from the

---

152   *The Myths of Mexico and Peru* by Lewis Spence. 1913 (2005). Barnes and Noble Books. Pg 165.
153   *The Myths of Mexico and Peru* by Lewis Spence. 1913 (2005). Barnes and Noble Books. Pg 136.
154   "A Peninsula That May Have Been an Island: Tayasal, Peten, Guatemala" by Ruben E. Reina. In the journal *Expedition*, Fall 1966. Pg 16 - 29. Accessed online at:
http://www.penn.museum/documents/publications/expedition/PDFs/9-1/Reina.pdf

Lowlands, where it was once the tongue of the mighty city-state of Chichén Itzá, the language still retains greater similarities to the Lowland languages than it does to its neighboring Mayan dialects, which suggests evidence of ancient migrations that occurred after the fall of Chichén Itzá.[155]

So what can be said with certainty about the disappearance of Chichén Itzá? The city was founded and located based upon long-distance trade in commodities and ideas, and when those networks collapsed after the destruction of both Tula and El Tajín, the city quickly lost a lot of its relevance. As trade moved in new directions, the wealthy families of the confederacy - the Cocomes and Xiu in particular - were forced to rely upon different sources of power and wealth, placing their emphasis on holdings outside the city. By 1220, about 50 years after the fall of Tula, the center of power was already at Mayapán. This was probably a period of strife between elite families seeking to maintain (or increase) their power in a shifting political and economic landscape, and this may explain why elites like Canek retreated up into the Highlands to establish a new Itzá city on the shores of Lake Petén Itzá. The old city was never completely abandoned, as it continued to be used for ritual purposes until the arrival of the Spanish, but it slowly faded with fewer and fewer families living in what was increasingly a ruin swallowed up by the jungle.

Even still, the last non-Catholicized Maya group, the Lacandon of Chiapas, regularly traveled to the nearby ruin of Bonampak, where they performed rituals within the ancient, ruined temples. This suggests they had an unbroken tradition of prayer and ritual that dated back to the time when the city was inhabited[156]. Likewise, there are accounts of the ruins of Uxmal being used by the powerful Xiu family (said to be descendants of the former rulers) and rituals occuring at Chichén Itzá even after the Spanish Conquest. Presumably, they took a form similar to that of the Lacandon: reverential entry into a site associated with both gods and ancestors, and then sacrifices and prayers made in crumbling temples and altars. It's possible the ruined state of the buildings became integrated into the religious lore itself, with the buildings becoming associated with a golden age of mythic ancestors worthy of veneration. In fact, Bishop Landa, the Spaniard sent to Christianize the Maya, ordered a cannon (and probably guards) to be placed on top of El Castillo to prevent just such activity.

Thus, even though Chichén Itzá declined, it continued to be a part of the sacred landscape and then bécame a landscape of folklore. In other words, Chichén Itzá never vanished from the Yucatec Mayan memory. During the "Talking Cross" revolts, part of the larger Mayan Caste War (1847-1901) against Mestizo domination, prophecies held that the rise of the revolt must include the rebels "reaching an agreement with the governor who lives in the ruins," an idea which was "a reference to the legendary Itzá king promised in the books of *Chilam Balam*"[157].

Regardless of the cause that brought about the revolt against Chichén, it appears that bitterness had been growing for some time. The smaller cities and towns, built in the old Puuc style, were ripe for a revolt in the name of patriotism, and in 1221, they found their leader and their spark in the form of Hunac Ceel, the founder of the Cocom dynasty. The Cocom were originally the dominant one of the

---

155   "Itza': A Language of Guatemala" in the Ethnologue. Accessed online at: http://www.ethnologue.com/language/itz
156   *Life, Ritual ánd Religion Among the Lacandon Maya* by R. Jon McGee (1990). Wadsworth Publishing.
157   *The Caste War of the Yucatán* by Nelson A. Reed (2001). Stanford University Press. Pg 154.

two lineages in the post-Chichén landscape and went on to become the founders of Mayapán. The family was founded by Hunac Ceel Cauich, an ethnic Mayan general who conquered the city of Chichén Itzá. During the conflict, Hunac Ceel was captured and eventually sacrificed to the god Chaac by being thrown into a cenote outside the city, but he survived in the cold waters all night and emerged the next day claiming to have a prophecy from Chaac himself. When his prophecy came true the following year, he was appointed by Chichén Itzá's rulers to become the ruler of Mayapán, which was at that point a tribute city of Chichén Itzá officially under the power of Ah Mex Cuc, Chichén's titular ruler.

If Ah Mex Cuc and the Itzáes (as the elites of the city were called) hoped that this would serve to remove him from an influential role over their city's politics, they were apparently grossly mistaken. Using Mayapán as a base, Hunac Ceel forged an alliance with Uxmal - another important Chichén Itzá tribute city - and conquered the great capital. With this stunning victory, he broke the chokehold of the Itzáes' council over local politics and established Mayapán as the capital of a new confederation including Mayapán, Uxmal and Chichén Itzá (sans the Ah Mex Cuc and the Itzáes' councilors)[158].

Recent archaeology shows that a settlement had previously existed at the location of Mayapán, which makes sense because its water sources would have allowed for agriculture, but the previous settlement was not a significant city, and certainly not a walled city or a capital before this time. The remnants of the Itzáes would flee the Yucatan altogether, retreating to Lake Peten Itzá in the Highlands of Guatemala, where their leaders would found another city called Tayasal that would be the last Mayan city to fall to the Spaniards[159]. At the same time, the political entity that emerged in the Yucatan - called the League of Mayapán - owed its structure to the political council of Chichén Itzá; the system was called Mul Tepal ("joint rule"). This relative equality between city-states in the League allowed for a structure to the Cocom-Xiu rivalry.

While the traditional texts, particularly the *Chilam Balam* manuscript, describe both Ah Mex Cuc and Hunac Ceel as "Itzáes," the ruling ethnic group of Chichén Itzá, it is tempting to see the conquest of Hunac Ceel as an example of an anti-foreigner indigenous uprising. The cities and towns that allied with Hunac Ceel (except for Uxmal) were all located around the Puuc Hills, a low mountain range in the Yucatan's northwest that had been a center for political and artistic power before the rise of Chichén Itzá. Moreover, one of the most notable cultural elements of Chichén Itzá in the Mayan landscape was its cosmopolitan character, so it certainly would have been associated with foreign ideas and foreign power during its time, perhaps even seen as an imperial intrusion on the landscape. Hunac Ceel's conquest of the city and his transfer of political and military power to Mayapán and its Puuc allies may have been seen as a return to traditional power structures and values.

Beyond the textual evidence, there are several other areas of interest for this thesis. First is the fact that Hunac Ceel replaced the Toltec-inspired ruling council of Chichén Itzá with a dynastic system led by his family, the Cocomes, which was similar to pre-Chichén Classic Mayan polities like Tikal (which

---

158   "Chapter 2: The Rise of Hunac Ceel to Power" from the *Chilam Balam* accessed online at:
       http://www.bibliotecapleyades.net/chilam_balam/cbc07.htm
159   *The Myths of Mexico and Peru* by Lewis Spence. 1913 (2005). Barnes and Noble Books. Pg 136.

may have been looked at as a Mayan Golden Age by Postclassic Yucatecans). Second is the fact that in Mayapán there was a conscious revival of a pre-Chichén architectural style called the Puuc Style, as well as other artistic forms like carved stones called stelae in distinctive traditional style called katun-ending.[160] Finally, the alliance went out of its way to recruit Uxmal, famous even today as a center of the Puuc Style and the previously dominant power before Chichén. At that point, Uxmal was probably a shadow of its former glory because no major construction had occurred at the site since the rise of Chichén.

At the same time, it also appears that the Cocomes were never fully confident of their own power, perhaps initially because they feared the return to power by the Itzáes at Chichén. Thus, instead of having a sprawling city like Chichén or Cobá (another contemporary city to the east), they built a densely packed walled city, something that had not been seen before in the Mayan world. The *Chilam Balam* even refers to Mayapán as "the Fortress." Such an expenditure of wealth needed to construct the city's mighty walls would not have been done lightly, providing further proof of a profound, long-term anxiety on the part of the city's rulers.

The Cocomes great rivals, the Tutul Xiu family (usually just called the Xius), were based in the city of Maní, which was listed in *Chilam Balam* as one of the allied towns within Hunac Ceel's original confederacy. The Xiu were originally rulers of Uxmal, which was the last flowering of the Classic Mayan civilization, and built upon the local base of the Puuc aesthetic, Uxmal reached its zenith under the only ruler commemorated in stone at the site: Lord Chaak. Rising up between 875 and 900 CE, Chaak seized the helm of Uxmal (previously governed by a council of elites) and forged it into a military power that quickly dominated its rivals. Under Chaak and his immediate successors, Uxmal expanded and built impressive structures, including a central pyramid called the Temple of the Magician. The temples here were focused upon the worship of the rain god Chaac. However, the era of glory was short-lived with the great palaces and temples abandoned by 925 CE, and while it appears that the city was not completely abandoned (it was inhabited during the time of Hunac Ceel 300 years later), it was eventually replaced in its position of regional dominance by Chichén[161].

160   "Survival and Revival of Terminal Classic Traditions at Postclassic Mayapán" by Susan Milbrath and Carlos Peraza Lope (2009). In the journal *Latin American Antiquity* 20(4) 581-606 accessed online at:
        http://www.jstor.org/discover/10.2307/40650048?uid=3739832&uid=2&uid=4&uid=3739256&sid=21103263281091
161   "Uxmal" in *Exploring Mesoamerica* by John M.D. Pohl (1999). Oxford University Press. Pgs 106-117.

A depiction of Chaac at Mayapán

When Uxmal returned to the historical record in the 1220s, during Hunac Ceel's rise, it was associated with a powerful noble family called the Xius. While it there is not a direct textual connection between Lord Chaak and the Xius, the family made a claim to the site and considered its abandoned temples to be theirs until the period of the Spanish Conquest. It appears that they were forced out of the city in the 13th century, after which they founded Maní, a smaller town[162]. Maní is still occupied today and was one of the centers for colonial power and the site of the first Franciscan mission in the region. Thus, while the Cocomes may have represented the new order founded by the charismatic and divinely inspired Hunac Ceel, the Xiu may have represented the old order of pre-Chichén Puuc glory, based in Uxmal and tracing its history back centuries to Lord Chaak, the last of the Classic Mayan kings and a towering historic figure that rivaled Hunac Ceel.

This balance of power between the two families remained in place for a little over two centuries until the fall of Mayapán in 1441 CE, when the Xius finally deposed their rivals and became the most powerful family of the region. By then, the original fear of the Itzá among the Cocom had probably been replaced by fear of the Xiu, and the eventual conquest of the city, despite the massive walls, shows that this fear was well-placed. The Xius, perhaps learning a lesson of the escape of the Itzáes from the fall of Chichén, butchered the Cocomes and drove the lone survivor (who was absent during the attack) into exile, obliterating the rival line with a single stroke. The justifications for the Xiu's actions were recorded by their eventual Spanish allies: "...the governing Cocom began to covet riches, and to that end negotiated with the garrison kept by the kings of Mexico [the Aztecs] in Tabasco and Xicalango, that he would put the city in their charge. In this way he introduced the Mexicans into

162   "Uxmal" at the *Encyclopedia Britannic Online.* Accessed online at:
       http://www.britannica.com/EBchecked/topic/620988/Uxmal#ref225522

Mayapán, oppressed the poor and made slaves of the many. [...] This Cocom was the first who made slaves; but out of this evil came the use of arms to defend themselves, that they might not all become slaves."[163]

This explanation should be taken with the same grain of salt that any post-facto justification of war needs, but it does give readers insight into what the Xius believed to be legitimate reasons for their wars. In particular, it is interesting that the chronicles repeatedly note in other sections the use of Mexican mercenaries by the Cocom to defend their position. Between the construction of walls and the importation of foreign mercenaries, it appears that the Cocom felt their precariousness long before their fall and attempted to stave off the Xius, but in the end it was all for naught: "The chiefs [of other cities] then attached themselves to the party of the Tutul-xiu, a man patriotic like his ancestors[164], and they plotted to kill Cocom. This they did, killing at the same time all of his sons save one who was absent; they sacked his dwelling and possessed themselves of all his property, his stores of cacao and other fruits, saying thus that they repaid themselves what had been stolen from them.[165]"

However, despite the aspirations of Xius to dominate the region, the post-Mayapán Yucatan did not become a Xiu-dominated confederacy centered on Maní. Instead, it increasingly fractured into small, warring statelets until the arrival of the Spanish, who did not encounter any unified resistance in the region. In fact, the Xius, in a last attempt for dominance, quickly allied with the Spanish, even inviting the Franciscan missionaries to live in Maní. Their plans would not work, and they, like all the other indigenous elites in Mesoamerica, were eventually dispossessed and replaced by Spaniards.

Chapter 5: The Layout of Mayapán

---

163   *Yucatan Before and After the Conquest* by Friar Diego de Landa. William Gates (trans.) 1566 (1978). Dover Books. Pg 15-16
164   Perhaps this is a reference to the Xiu's previous participation in Hunac Ceel's alliance to oust the Itzaes.
165   *Ibid*

A view of Mayapán from one of its pyramids. Photo by Marie-Christine Ferland

Mayapán was a dense city compared to the sprawling metropolises of the Classic period. Within its walls, 4,000 buildings were clustered in an area of 4.2 square kilometers (1.5 square miles), and original estimates of over 10,000 inhabitants have been recently bumped up to a population of 15,000-17,000. While this may not be large for a modern settlement, it was a considerable town for the Mayan Postclassic period after Chichén, and it had all the features one would expect in a power base, including walls, temples, plazas, palaces and markets. Altogether, The layout of the city walls created an area that has a rough appearance of the outline of a pick-ax head. Using this metaphor, the "blade" of the pick-ax faces west and southwest, and the pick juts off to the northeast. The city's center was located in the western third of the city, near the "axe-blade" of the pick-ax.

Ruins of Mayapán's walls

At the center of this "blade" was the main plaza, the location of the most important buildings, including palaces, central plazas, temples and other ritual structures. The most important structure is the Temple of the god Kukulcán, located on the south side of the central plaza. Decorated with pillars covered in plumed serpents; it is a smaller version of the famous "Castillo" (also a temple to Kukulcán) of Chichén Itzá.

On the east side of the same plaza was the second tallest pyramid, today called "Crematorio" or "Crematorium", and across the plaza is another little brother of a famous Chichén structure: the Templo Redondo, which mimics the larger city's Caracol celestial observatory.[166] This Plaza would have served many purposes, as it was probably officially for the populace to gather to observe important ceremonies on top of the pyramids, but since it was in the heart of the city, it would have been an important crossroads for the day-to-day traffic of commerce, governance and socialization.

166   "Zona Arqueológica de Mayapán" in the website Conaculta, of the INAH. Accessed online at:
       http://www.inah.gob.mx/english-press-releases/44-lista-de-zonas-arqueologicas/6042-zona-arqueologica-de-mayapan

Photos by Joel De Salvatierra

Surrounding the plaza were the workshops and potentially homes of the city's many craftspeople, but immediately to the east and west of their workshops are the palaces of the most powerful families. Undoubtedly both the Cocom and Xiu had mansions here, and though it's tempting to place the dominant Cocom in a particularly large palace directly to the west of the plaza and set within its own semi-agricultural fields, there's no evidence confirming this was their mini-estate within the city. The four or five remaining palaces that have been discovered are located to the east of the plaza and are surrounded by residential neighborhoods, including the smaller palaces presumably owned by lesser nobility. Historians know that the League of Mayapán confederacy that emerged out of Hunac Ceel's revolution involved a council of leaders dominated by a small number of families, and given this knowledge, many imagine each of these palaces were possibly the "city homes" for families with greater estates in their own city-state elsewhere in the Yucatan. It's possible that like the great capitals of Europe, there was a courtly season when these houses were filled and the social rounds and politicking were intense, followed by a period when the families retired to their ancestral estates[167].

To the north of this residential zone, close to the north wall (and the top of the "ax-head") was the city's principal marketplace, a sprawling area perhaps larger than the Main Plaza. This market edged the main highway to the north, which in turn led to the Main Plaza and from there to the south and southeast gates.

Despite the density of the settlement, the interior of the walls was dotted with *milpas*, the local term for corn and vegetable fields. 23 agricultural fields have been found within the walls, and a further 14 in the immediate vicinity, within sight of the fortifications. These areas may have meant that the city could have withstood sieges longer by producing their own food, and they may also have served as "truck gardens," providing the daily fruits and vegetables for the city's market.

In addition to the grand temples at the city's heart, there were smaller temple complexes scattered throughout the grounds. For instance, recent excavations in the northeast of the city have found the Itzmal Ch'en ceremonial group, including a small pyramid temple, and three priests' buildings flanking a small plaza with a cenote (sinkhole well) in its center[168]. They have also found a mass grave containing 18 elite patrons of the temple[169].

While Mayapán attracts droves of curious tourists, the most defining feature of the city for the Maya was its defensive walls. While the name "Mayapán" signifies "The Banner of the Maya"[170], Spanish chronicler Diego de Landa noted that the city had another, more common name: "Ich-pa" ("within the fortifications")[171]. The importance of these walls for the city's place in the Mayan imagination is further reinforced by the *Chilam Balam* text, which refers to the city as "the Fortress." The only similarly

---

167   "2001-2009 Seasons: 60 Contexts in 36 Milpa Fields (surface collection, test pits) 11 fully excavated structures." accessed online at: http://lh4.ggpht.com/-
alnkTk6O19o/TYYD9NKxW7I/AAAAAAAAAXg/6ovE5V9aI84/s800/Slide2.JPG
168   This site may be connected to the great Postclassic pilgrimage site called Itzmal on the island of Cozumel, much in the way that Catholic hospitals and churches around the world are named after the pilgrimage site of Lourdes.
169   *Postclassic Maya Settlement on the Rural-Urban Fringe of Mayapan, Yucatan* by Bradley W. Russell. Accessed online at: http://books.google.com/books?id=fzt-
wIr8zb8C&pg=PR49&lpg=PR49&dq=Itzmal+Ch%27en+mayapan&source=bl&ots=bBU2eB1nlB&sig=2fl-
TBhUIT_9TXbx7mT34cdiPDc&hl=en&sa=X&ei=_YnhUvX8EdLMsQS3m4C4BQ&ved=0CCUQ6AEwAA#v=onepag
e&q=Itzmal%20Ch%27en%20mayapan&f=false
170   "Zona Arqueológica de Mayapán" in the website Conaculta, of the INAH. Accessed online at:
http://www.inah.gob.mx/english-press-releases/44-lista-de-zonas-arqueologicas/6042-zona-arqueologica-de-mayapan
171   *Yucatan Before and After the Conquest* by Friar Diego de Landa. William Gates (trans.) 1566 (1978). Dover Books. Pg 11

walled town in the Yucatan was the little fortified port-town of Tulum on the eastern shore, which is today immensely popular among tourists in Cancún. The walls have been estimated to be 9 kilometers (over 5.5 miles) long, 10-15 feet thick, and over 6 feet high, with a parapet on top[172]. The walls were guarded by 12 gates, seven of which were major entrances with vaulted chambers, and the gates were scattered with some regularity around the walls.[173] Three gates have temples just inside them and the gates are also sometimes close to cenotes. The number and placement of the gates was probably for the ease not only of long-distance trade but also for farmers who lived within the walls to have easy access to their fields, as well as for similar economic activities like firewood gathering and hunting. Archaeologists have found that some of these gates were blocked, so it is probable that only a portion of the gates were functioning at any given time, but it is also possible that they were blocked up in the city's final days as a way to forestall entry by the armies of the Xiu.

Chapter 6: Life in Mayapán

Like Chichén Itzá before it, Mayapán was a cosmopolitan city full of nobility and foreigners, thanks to the fact it inherited the remnants of the earlier city's trade empire, including the ports at Cozumel and Xicalango and trade routes into modern-day Honduras and central Mexico. The city's elite also continued the tradition of adopting many Mexican religious and courtly traditions, and they apparently relied heavily on a large number of Mexican mercenaries who lived in the city in its last years. As a result, a visit to the "Fortress" would have been a thrilling one for travelers from the smaller hinterland towns, who could encounter all sorts of exotic goods, religions and individuals[174].

Both the city and the fragmented outlying towns that preceded it and survived it were strictly divided between the ruling class and the peasantry, so even though the Yucatecans by and large did not practice the Classical Mayan tradition of divine kingship, they still maintained a rigid caste system. This wasn't lost on anyone in Mayapán either, since the nobility had grand palaces of varying size within the city. While the extravagance of the noble lifestyle probably declined after the abandonment of Mayapán, the Spanish left an impression of some of their diversions: "They often spend on one banquet all they have made by many days of trading and scheming. They have two methods of making these feasts; [...] that of the chiefs and leading men obliges each guest to return an invitation to his host; to each guest the host must give a roast fowl and cacao and drinks in abundance, and after the banquet it is custom to present each with a small mantle to wear, with a small stand and a cup as fine as the host can afford."[175]

At the feasts, they were entertained by jesters "who perform with great skill," and musicians who played various types of wooden drums, tortoise rattles, bone whistles, conch shells, and reed flutes. These musicians often accompanied dancers, with dances being done among single-gender groups. One included the "colomché" ("palisade of sticks"), where large circles of dancers moves in time to

---

172   *The Carnegie Maya Series Ebook* by John M. Weeks (ed). By the University Press of Colorado. Pg XXI
173   "All structures with Carnegie map" at the *Maya Periphery Project* accessed online at:
       http://mayapanperiphery.net/images/maps/Structures-All_with_Carnegie_Map_Limits.jpg
174   "Life at the Ancient City" from *Mayapán Archaeology* accessed online at: http://www.albany.edu/mayapan/life-at-
       the-ancient-city.shtml
175   *Yucatan Before and After the Conquest* by Friar Diego de Landa. William Gates (trans.) 1566 (1978). Dover
       Books. Pgs 35-37

drums while two dancers enter the center of the circle and toss reed sticks at each other, catching them with grace. Another dance involved roughly 800 dancers bearing flags that lasted for an entire day, with dancers eating and drinking while moving to the time of the music[176]. In contrast to the nobility, the commoners had more restrained festivals, "...when they marry their children or celebrate the deeds of their ancestors. This does not have to be returned...[177]"

In addition to these openly festive occasions, Mayapán was also undoubtedly the site of elaborate religious and courtly performances of various types. These dramas often involved blood sacrifices; worshipers typically offered some of their own blood, but at important times the lives of captured prisoners purchased by elite families were offered instead. Scholars have only a rough idea of the ceremony involved, because the Spanish were primarily interested in recording details of the blood sacrifice itself and comprehensively destroyed other religious texts[178]. However, a small glimpse into the world of this colorful pageantry is available in the form of the Rabinal Achí Ballet of the Guatemala Highlands. Each year, in the village of Kajyub', performers gather in incredible masked costumes portraying figures from the ancient dynastic past and re-creating historic events in dramatic fashion for the crowds. The positions of the performers and musicians are inherited from one generation to the next, and neither script nor music is written down, as it is a form of patrimony passed down orally[179]. While the Highlanders of Guatemala are of a different branch of the Mayan culture family tree, scholars surmise that similar dramas - perhaps depicting the lives of figures like Lord Chaak or Hunac Ceel - played a central role in the life of the city. They would have served to legitimize the leadership roles of the descendants of the figures depicted and explain the city's unique place to the general public.

When Mayapán was at its height, it's easy to envision the constant round of ceremonial offerings, historical dance-dramas and reciprocal noble feasts with accompanying gifts. Undoubtedly, they would have supported an entire economy of craftspeople producing mantles, stands, cups, reed sticks and dance flags, as well as the formal attire, body decoration and jewelry, and the various food and drink consumed. There may also have been a slave market, where military prisoners could be purchased by wealthy families for service in their homes and estates or as offerings to the gods.

In the warm climate of the Yucatan, elaborate clothing was not necessary for protection from the elements, and the everyday garb of Mayan commoners was relatively simple. The Spanish missionary Diego de Landa described men as wearing little more than a breechcloth: a cotton belt with a strip of cloth tucked into the front, passed between the legs and tucked into the back so that its ends hung down. These were often embroidered or decorated with colorful feathers. The women wore a bit more, donning square cotton mantles that were similarly decorated. Mayan women of the region today are renowned for their beautifully embroidered cotton gowns, called *huipils*, which may be similar to the mantles of this period[180]. On their feet they wore sandals of deerskin or hemp.

---

176   *Ibid*
177   *Ibid*
178   *Yucatan Before and After the Conquest* by Friar Diego de Landa. William Gates (trans.) 1566 (1978). Dover Books. Pgs 47-49
179   "The Rabinal Achí Dance Drama" at the *UNESCO Oral and Intangible Heritage of Humanity* Website, accessed online at: http://www.unesco.org/culture/intangible-heritage/15lac_uk.htm
180   "The Huipil" at *Images of the Maya*. Accessed online at: http://www.flmnh.ufl.edu/maya/maya5.htm

The lack of complicated outfits was made up for with body modification and temporary decorations, including piercings, tattoos, filed teeth and "coiffures as fine as those of the most coquettish Spanish women." The basic outfits of the elites were the same, though they appear to have added elaborate headdresses and jewelry, at least in ceremonial occasions. This description has been confirmed by comparisons to surviving frescoes in buildings and Mayan books.[181] Despite the overall similarity of attire amongst the social classes, there was almost certainly an elaborate gradation of decoration and quality which separated not only the nobles from the commoners but the well-to-do of each caste from those who were struggling. Since the city possessed widespread trade routes, it is probable that the finer attire was in part marked by its use of rare imported goods, such as turquoise from the deserts of the modern-day American Southwest. In the modern Guatemalan Mayan market town of Chichicastenango, various Mayan communities are marked by their distinctive, colorful woven styles, creating a riot of color which can be read by knowledgeable actors[182], and the market of Mayapán was likely the same. Different types of outfits would have been appropriate for various social and labor contexts, and for certain weather conditions. While much of the detail will always remain conjectural, beautiful and evocative attempts at reconstruction can stir inspiration[183].

As noted above, the city was dotted with *milpa* gardens and surrounded by an agricultural belt. Taken in conjunction with each other, this meant that the majority of the city's food sources were undoubtedly obtained fresh from the immediate area. Because the Native Americans did not have beasts of burden outside of the Andes, it would have been inefficient to transport even dried corn over long distances, as the bearers would eventually need to eat more than what they carried. This means that the populations of Mesoamerican cities were largely confined by what was possible to grow in their immediate surroundings, like an island of agriculture around a fixed water source. Hence, growth was typically accomplished by conquering other city-islands or affiliating them in a great confederacy, as was the case with Mayapán

As a result, the diet of the city could be divided into two elements: the majority of goods produced locally and a minority of imported goods which were brought in by trade used by the elites or for ceremonial occasions. At the heart of the diet - whether rich or poor, male or female - was corn grown in the milpas. Contemporary Yucatecan Maya also rely heavily upon the plant in tortillas, tamales and drinks, but with that said, the diets were relatively more varied than in the Classic Period, when population pressures had forced the Maya to rely almost entirely upon corn.[184] Another important plant was cacao, which served as a form of currency, and the Mayans also consumed chili peppers, squash, runner beans, peanuts, tomatoes, avocado, vanilla, sunflowers, and fruits like sapote and papaya[185].

181   *Yucatan Before and After the Conquest* by Friar Diego de Landa. William Gates (trans.) 1566 (1978). Dover Books. Pgs 33, 53-54
182   *Chichicastenango: A Guatemalan Village* by Ruth Leah Bunzel (1967). University of Washington Press.
183   A great example is the "Lowland Maya Postclassic Fashion Set" by an artist known as "Plumed Serpent." It is available on the website DeviantArt: http://plumed-serpent.deviantart.com/art/Lowland-Maya-Postclassic-Fashion-Set-343999681
184   "Dental caries at a late pre-Hispanic regional Maya capital" by S. Serafin (2010) in *HOMO- Journal of Comparative Human Biology.* V 61, I 3, pp. 217-218
185   "Mesoamerican Plants and Foods" accessed online at: http://clio.missouristate.edu/chuchiak/New%20Webpage%20Images/HST%20397---Theme%205---Mesoamerican_plants_and_foods.htm

Archaeologists have found that the ruins have a disproportionate number of tall Standley Cactus, which were apparently planted by the ancients for its edible fruit and the fact that its flesh can be used in the production of arrow shafts.[186]. It would have been a rich diet, especially at the hands of trained chefs.

The people of the city ate a number of wild animals, including white-tailed deer, iguana, peccary and brocket deer, but they also had a handful of domesticated animals, like turkeys and dogs. This paucity of domesticated species is not strange because the Americas were not blessed with the wide array of domesticatable animals found in the Old World. In addition to dogs and turkeys, the only other animals were South American ones like the llama, alpaca, guinea pig, and Muscovy duck. In addition to these local foods, the city imported some exotic meats and seafood, which (along with dog meat) joined the venison on the tables of leaders.

Studies have found that the amount of white-tailed deer consumed within the city was beyond what should have been available to normal hunting, so some have speculated that either the people of Mayapán created an enclosed deer park or otherwise manipulated the nearby forest to encourage deer. White-tailed deer was considered a high-status food and was regularly consumed by the city's elites, and deer meat and bones were both important trade goods. The skulls of the deer were ritually disposed of in a way different from other meats, further setting apart the importance of venison[187].

Chapter 7: Outside the Walls

Early studies of Mayapán focused upon the ceremonial center and based their population estimates on the number of buildings within the walls, but recent work has shown that while the formal city may have ended at the gates, the economic and social world of the city expanded beyond it into the surrounding landscape. In the agricultural "island" that supported the city just beyond its walls, there were a number of informal settlements based around colonnaded customs buildings near the major gates - one in the southwest, one in the center on the north, the center of the wall on the south, and the east, southeast and northeast corners. These settlements appear to have been built along the highways leading up to the gates and taper off past 500 meters from the walls[188].

One exception was a small settlement outside the 500 meter band. Along the southern highway was a settlement that contained a small marketplace, the only one discovered outside of the main market in the north of the city thus far. Scholars can only speculate as to why this market existed, but it is possible that its location outside of the gates of the city allowed merchants to avoid gate taxes or trading rules within the city. If that was the case, it's hard to understand why the authorities in Mayapán would permit this market to exist, but whatever the reason, it apparently had a special exception for reasons lost to history.

One of the most important features of the city's surrounding landscape were the sacred cenotes, which

---

186   A picture of Dr. Clifford T. Brown with a Standley Cactus and an explanation of their role can be found here:
       https://sites.google.com/site/mayaarchaeology/
187   "Animal Use at the Postclassic Maya center of Mayapán" by Marilyn A. Masson and Carlos Peraza Lopez (2008)
       in the journal *Quaternary International* 191: 170-183
188   "New Site Limits 500 M" at the *Mayapan Periphery Project* accessed online at:
       http://mayapanperiphery.net/images/maps/New-Site-Limits-500m.jpg

were sinkholes that opened up to precious underground water sources. The Maya considered cenotes to be holy spaces that allowed for interaction with the sacred realm of the gods. It was for this reason that Hunac Ceel was sacrificed by being thrown into the cenote, and why he was considered to have been touched by the god Chaac when he emerged alive. Despite the lush nature of the Yucatan jungle, for agriculturalists it is akin to a desert. There are almost no surface sources of water, so all hydration must come up from underground sources. The area around the city contained at least 100 documented holes, but not all were usable for agriculture. Researchers have begun to explore inside Mayapán's cenotes, which contain ceramics, burials and other ritual activities.[189] Over 20 bodies have been found in them as well.[190]

A visitor approaching the city at its height would not have necessarily seen the subterranean cenotes or taken much notice of the small market town to the south of the city, but what would have dominated the immediate area surrounding the city were the milpas and the attendant farms. While today it is tough to imagine Mayapán crowded by the jungle, recent work in the Mayapán Periphery Project has found that the city was surrounded by an extensive band of agriculture and settlement, with many farmers living just outside the city walls. Agricultural fields, probably growing corn amongst other crops, extended outwards, while to the north was a livestock production area, perhaps dedicated to semi-domesticated white-tailed deer. Furthermore, the post-Mayapán rural Yucatecans' daily lives were described by Diego de Landa. In his text, *Yucatan Before and After the Conquest*, he describes rural farmers as living within whitewashed wooden homes built with steeply-pitched roofs. They worked both their own fields and in the fields of local elites with their neighbors. In these *milpa*, they primarily grew corn (maize), as well as chili peppers and other vegetables, and they gained much of their protein from hunting.[191]

Beyond even the milpas was the forest, the dense jungles of the Yucatan that would eventually swallow the city's ruins. The transition from field to forest would not have been immediate, because the Maya like studded the forest with milpas within walking distance wherever fertility and water made agriculture possible. Additionally, the nearby forests would have been more akin to a managed landscape than a wild one, with city dwellers utilizing it heavily for wild products. These included not only the white-tailed deer but also wood for cooking fires, honey from the stingless Yucatecan bees, other meats like peccary, and numerous wild vegetables, fruits, tubers and herbs.

Chapter 8: The Centrality of Religion in Mayapán

Like any great capital, religious life in Mayapán was incredibly rich and varied. The city was dotted with temples, and it also served as a place of both religious innovation and older traditions. For example, around 1300 or 1325, the city's residents developed a new type of ritual object called a Chen

---

189   "In the Jaws of the Earth: Getting to the Bottom of Ancient Mayapán, Mexico" by Bradley Russell for *National Geographic* (2013). Accessed online at: http://newswatch.nationalgeographic.com/2013/08/01/in-the-jaws-of-the-earth-getting-to-the-bottom-of-ancient-mayapan-mexico/

190   "Returning Maya Ancestors to their Place of Origin" at *Past Horizons* 2 September 2013. Accessed online at: http://www.pasthorizonspr.com/index.php/archives/09/2013/returning-maya-ancestors-to-their-place-of-origin

191   *Yucatan Before and After the Conquest* by Friar Diego de Landa. William Gates (trans.) 1566 (1978). Dover Books. Pgs 32-39, 93-101

Mul effigy incense burner, in which they burned copal incense as a technique for contacting the gods. This was a new way of interacting with the various Mayan deities, and clearly an important religious development[192], but the shifting roles of two key gods also demonstrate how the religion in the city morphed. The two most notable examples were Kukulcán, a god imported from the Toltecs via Chichén Itzá, and the second being the ancient Mayan god Chaac. While many of the details are lost, these two gods appeared to be closely connected to the political currents that swept up both Mayapán and Chichén Itzá.

The Maya had long possessed their own well-organized and elaborate religious world. While it is true that they had a number of religious characteristics - worship at pyramidal temples, blood sacrifice and a rich polytheism - that came from a pan-Mesoamerican religious tradition, there was much that made the Mayan religion distinctive, much the same way that the Abrahamic faiths (Christianity, Judaism, and Islam) share several similar features but retain their own distinct character. One uniquely Mayan god was Chaac (also spelled "Chac" or "Chaak"), who was a deity of rain, fertility, agriculture, thunder and rain. A beloved deity, Chaac was a protector of humanity and taught his worshipers how to grow crops. He was also associated with frogs, who were said to be his servants and hailed the coming of his storms with their croaks. Chaac was traditionally depicted as having fangs and an upturned proboscis-like nose, but as the Mayan religious tradition in the Yucatan evolved, Chaac was seen as served by many minor rain gods (also called chaacs), and he became known as one of the Bacabs, one of four protective deities associated with the cardinal points of the compass (with Chaac representing the east).[193]

It's easy to understand why a rain deity would be so important, give that agriculture is famously difficult in the Yucatan. Farmers must rely upon subsurface waters drawn from cenotes and by the rare and precious rains. In this context, Chaac appears to have emerged as the dominant deity of the Puuc city-states, and Uxmal in particular is renowned for its temples lavishly festooned with stone Chaac masks.[194] Chaac was of such great importance that modern-day traditional priests called "h-men" in the northern Yucatan - living amongst the ruins of the Puuc cities - continue to venerate the god[195]. In rituals held in the ruins of Cobá and the modern city of Mérida, the h-men made offerings of pigs to Chaac, as well as various Catholic saints, but explained that in previous times it was done using venison - probably similar to the offerings made in ancient Mayapán.

The relatively stable Chaac-centered religious life of Puuc was fundamentally changed during the dominance of Chichén Itzá in the Yucatan. Amongst other cultural elements imported from the Toltecs of Central Mexico was a new religious cult dedicated to worshiping the god Kukulcán. Kukulcán, the sovereign feathered serpent deity, became incredibly popular during this time, and Chichén Itzá became a center for pilgrimage and worship, with visitors coming from all over the Mayan world.[196]

---

192   "Mayapán's Effigy Censers: Iconography, Context, and External Connections" by, Carlos Peraza Lope, Centro INAH Yucatán (2007). Accessed online at: http://www.famsi.org/reports/05025/index.html
193   "Chac" at the *Encyclopedia Mythica* by Henk Jan van Scheicoven (1997). Accessed online at: http://www.pantheon.org/articles/c/chac.html and "Chac" at the *Mythology Dictionary* (2012). Accessed online at: http://www.mythologydictionary.com/chac-mythology.html
194   Images of the Uxmal temples can be found at: http://www.canstockphoto.com/images-photos/uxmal.html
195   "The Mayas and Medicine" accessed online at: http://yucatantoday.com/en/topics/mayas-and-medicine

Much as the h-men of the Yucatan continue to venerate Chaak, the last non-Christianized Mayan group, the Lacandon of Chiapas, continue to worship Kukulcán, and they live in a region that is amongst the most distant corners of the Mayan-inhabited world[197]. In 1492, the cult of Kukulcán, which stretched throughout all of Mesoamerica, could have been considered one of the world's great proselytizing faiths, on par with Christianity or Buddhism.

Throughout (and despite) the dominance of Kukulcán, the Maya continued to venerate Chaac and their previous pantheon, a continuation that nobody in the region considered abnormal. Amongst the contemporaneous Aztec peoples, their local version of Kukulcán, called Quetzalcoatl, was worshiped alongside a rain god named Tlaloc, the war god Huitzilopochtli and many other deities[198]. However, there is some confusion in the historical record about the roles of the two gods in Mayapán and the post-Chichén political and religious domains. On the one hand, Chaac was undoubtedly at the center of the foundation of the new city, since Hunac Ceel received a vision in the sacred cenote of Chichén directly from Chaac, and it is in part on this divine blessing that the Cocom family based its legitimacy. They also went out of their way to recruit Uxmal and to emulate its Puuc style; both the city and its buildings are notable for their use of Chaac masks as one of the dominant decorative motifs. At the same time, worship of Kukulcán appears to have kept its central place in Yucatecan religious life, as the largest temple in Mayapán was dedicated to the Plumed Serpent and in essence was a small version of the great Castillo in Chichén Itzá. Tulum, a city founded during this period, was dominated by the Temple to the Wind God, dedicated to Kukulcán.[199] Even the Xiu, who based their power on Uxmal's legacy, worshiped Kukulcán, and when the Spanish arrived, they were renowned for their annual festival to the god, during which their tribute states brought offerings to the temples in Maní. The Spanish described a remarkable procession "with many comedians" and fasting that lasted for five days, until on the final day, the god Kukulcán himself descended the temple steps[200].

Moreover, there is a curious tale about the founding of Mayapán that has been passed down. The story told (presumably by his Xiu allies) to the Spanish priest Diego de Landa about the city's origin is that it was actually founded by Kukulcán, who first founded Chichén Itzá and then - after governing there for a time - moved to Mayapán, where he ruled until returning to Mexico[201]. While Landa was apparently an excellent Yucatecan speaker, it is probable that there is some confusion here. The High Priest of Kukulcán was also called "Kukulcán" and this probably means that once Mayapán displaced Chichén as the regional capital, the high priest was moved to the new temple. He says that only after this did the Cocomes come to power.

196   "Kukulkan" and "Quetzalcoatl" at the *Encyclopedia Mythica*. Accessed online at: http://www.pantheon.org/. "Kukulcan" at the *Mythology Dictionary*. Accessed online at: http://www.mythologydictionary.com/kukulcan-mythology.html
197   *Handbook of Mesoamerican Mythology* by Kay Almere Read and Jason González (2000). Oxford University Press. Pg 201
198   *Tenochtitlan: The History of the Aztec's Most Famous City* by Jesse Harasta (2013). Charles Rivers Editors.
199   "Zona Arqueológica de Tulum" at the National Institute of Anthropology and History of Mexico Homepage http://www.inah.gob.mx/index.php?option=com_content&view=article&id=5491
200   *Yucatan Before and After the Conquest* by Friar Diego de Landa. William Gates (trans.) 1566 (1978). Dover Books. Pg 74
201   *Yucatan Before and After the Conquest* by Friar Diego de Landa. William Gates (trans.) 1566 (1978). Dover Books. Pgs 9-11

Chapter 9: Mayapán's Decline

Given several centuries of retrospect, it's clear that the Xiu family has a terrible legacy of destruction to account for. They were on hand with the Cocomes to topple the Itzáes and bring mighty Chichén Itzá to its knees, and they were also riding in the vanguard of the alliance that eventually destroyed the Cocomes and the city of Mayapán. It is probable that the Xius did not intend to destroy Mayapán completely, but they apparently looted the city, vandalized certain artifacts, and moved whatever instruments of power they could back to Maní. Meanwhile, recent archaeology has shown that their victory in 1441 was quickly followed up by plague that caused the remaining families to flee the citadel[202]. Finally, they must bear some of the guilt for the chaos that succeeded the city's fall and the destruction that emerged from their eventual fateful alliance with the Spanish.

In the immediate aftermath of the fall of Mayapán, the most important effect was that the League of Mayapán was shattered with the city. Instead of being able to transfer authority to Maní, the Xiu found themselves once again as one family amongst many striving for power within the region. Of course, this doesn't mean that they didn't try to consolidate power. When the Spanish arrived, the largest festival to Kukulcán was held annually in Maní, which may have represented a legacy of the transfer of Kukulcán's priesthood to the Xiu town, the same priesthood that had been forced to leave Chichén two centuries earlier for Mayapán.

The century between the sack of Mayapán in 1441 and the Spanish Conquest of the region in 1542 was a dark period for the Yucatecans, as their former unity disintegrated into 16 rival statelets, each centered on a ritual center that was truly a glorified town compared to the old cities. While Mayapán, Uxmal and Chichén Itzá were never forgotten, they were largely abandoned and began their long conversion back into jungle. Uxmal and Chichén both remained important religious sites, but the priests probably lived alone in the ruins, much like some of the Medieval Popes for whom Rome was basically a collection of old churches and ecclesiastical buildings surrounded by a vast ruin.

It was into this balkanized landscape that the Spanish arrived. In his seminal book about the Americas before and after the arrival of Europeans, *1491: New Revelations of the Americas Before Columbus*[203], Charles C. Mann described a "master narrative" about the Conquest, struggling over the fact that almost everywhere across the Americas, indigenous groups facing the Europeans were decimated and conquered[204]. This "Master Narrative" has emerged out of historical, archaeological and ethnographic studies of numerous indigenous-European encounters, and Mann wrote that Conquest always occurred in the wake of two factors: widespread plague and the European exploitation of internal divisions amongst the indigenous peoples.

Not surprisingly, this model held true within the Yucatan. Despite the fact that Hernan Cortes, the conqueror of the Aztec Empire, visited the Mayan coastline on his journey to the heart of Mexico in 1521, the Spanish initially ignored the tiny Yucatecan statelets, because there seemingly weren't great

---

202   "Timeline" at Mayapán Archaeology. Accessed online at: http://www.albany.edu/mayapan/timeline.shtml

203   *1491: New Revelations of the Americas Before Columbus* by Charles C. Mann (2005). Knopf Publishers.

204   It should be noted that there are a few 'unconquered' peoples, including Amazonian groups like the Yanomamo and the Kayapó, the Seminoles of Florida and a handful of others.

prizes to be won there. Only after conquering the Aztecs and the Oaxacan Mixtec and Zapotec states did the Spanish return to the Yucatan. Here, however, the indigenous peoples put up strong resistance, and in some ways they have never been completely subjugated, as the modern Maya-based Zapatista revolt in Chiapas demonstrates. The first expedition to the Yucatan was led by a father-son team of Francisco de Montejo senior and junior. They invaded Mayan lands first in 1528 and then again in 1535. Finally, they managed to found a fortified coastal base in the town of Campeche in 1540 and succeeded in their interior campaign only after taking Maní in 1542 and effectively allying themselves to the Xiu. The last of the resistant Yucatecan polities were conquered by 1546[205]. The last independent Mayan state - the Highland Itzá stronghold of Tayasal - was finally brought to its knees in 1697.

205   *The Chronicle of the Mayan Kings and Queens: Deciphering the Dynasties of the Ancient Maya* by Simon Martin and Nikolai Grube (2000). Thames and Hudson. Pgs 229-230

A monument to the Montejo's in the city of Mérida in the Yucatan

Modern observers may ask why the Xius allied themselves to a foreign power that they likely knew had brought down the mighty Aztec empire. The problem, as Mann describes it, is that indigenous elites like the Xiu did recognize the power of the Spanish but attempted to utilize this new power for their own benefit. The Xiu had been attempting to dominate the Yucatan for centuries and were most likely deeply embittered by their failure to consolidate their control after the fall of Mayapán. The alliance between the Xius and the Spanish provided the opening that the de Montejo's had been seeking for years, and it was most likely very successful for the Xius as well at first because it allowed them a measure of dominance that they had only dreamed of.

While it was the de Montejo family of Conquistadores that broke the political and military power of the Yucatecan statelets, they did not break the cultural power of the Chichén-Puuc tradition. That would come later, with the arrival of Diego de Landa Calderón (1524-1579) to the Yucatan. Diego de Landa was sent to the Yucatan along with the first wave of Franciscan missionaries to the region in 1549. The Spanish crown had previously given the Franciscans a spiritual monopoly over the Yucatan, and de Landa pursued two goals during his tenure: (1) conversion of the Maya and (2) consolidation of the Franciscan power base.

A portrait of Diego de Landa Calderón

De Landa made quick inroads with the Xiu - his local power base - and then spread out across the conquered areas of the Yucatan, establishing mission posts and converting locals. However, it was not until 1562 that de Landa went from being a minor figure in history to one of the most notorious book burners and destroyers of religious tradition in human history. It was in this year that de Landa realized that the majority of the conversions that he had made were false ones and that the Maya, even his close allies, continued to worship their own gods in secret. He flew into a rage at this stunning betrayal of his life's work, and he and his aides scoured the Yucatan for books, codices, relics and ritual implements, which they gathered at the Xiu town of Maní. There, he gathered all of the assembled objects together and simultaneously burned them in a spectacular auto-de-fé, a term that means "act of faith," which was used to describe a public act of penance. He explained, "We found a large number of books in these characters and, as they contained nothing in which were not to be seen as superstition and lies of the devil, we burned them all, which they (the Maya) regretted to an amazing degree, and which caused them much affliction."

In some ways, this event was not out of the ordinary. The Spanish had used these events to burn accused witches for some time, and the Catholic Church burned religious objects in Mexico, Peru, Brazil and Goa. A very similar event had occurred in 1497 in Florence, Italy, when a Dominican priest named Girolama Savanarola convinced followers to burn objects associated with sins, including mirrors, fine clothing, gambling objects, books and secular music and art, during an event called the Bonfire of the Vanities.

Those predecessors aside, de Landa's actions were a largely unprecedented, shocking and heartbreaking event that effectively shattered centuries of religious, political, legal, poetic and artistic tradition. The destruction was so thorough that almost no written texts survived, an event of destruction far more extensive than Cortes' destruction of the Aztec court or the Sack of Rome by the Vandals, which both left considerable written legacies. Even de Landa's contemporaries recognized that his actions went beyond the norm; the bishop of the area sent him back to Spain to be held for trial for exceeding his authority. In the interregnum before his trial, he wrote a book entitled *Relación de las cosas de Yucatán* (roughly translated into English as *Yucatan Before and After the Conquest*) in 1566, in which he described the history, language, livelihoods, and religion of the Maya and defended his actions. In 1569, he was found innocent, and in 1571 he had returned to the Yucatan, now holding the position of Bishop[206].

While de Landa never fully succeeded in rooting out the "heresies" and "apostasies" that he saw under every rock - a distinctly Mayan form of religion continues to this very day - he and his contemporaries were effective in obliterating every element of Mayan elite and courtly life, to the point that what is known about the pre-Columbian period today is largely what they saw fit to preserve in their own books or what can be gleaned by archaeologists from shattered ruins. As a result, it can be said that the cultural tradition that began in the Puuc cities, matured in the beauty of Uxmal, rose to glory in Chichén Itzá, regrouped from the disaster of the fall of the Toltecs behind the safety of the walls of Mayapán, and survived even that refuge in the small Yucatecan states, finally ended in the fires of Maní. Stripped of their kings and priests and cities, the Maya did not vanish but instead

---

206   *Yucatan Before and After the Conquest* by Friar Diego de Landa. William Gates (trans.) 1566 (1978). Dover Books.

retreated into the jungles, where they remain today, a vibrant but humble people.

Chapter 10: The Rediscovery of the Cities' Ruins

The ancient Maya were "rediscovered" by the West in the mid-19th century when the writings of de Landa and other Spaniards came to the attention of an English-speaking public fascinated with the emerging field of archaeology. Eventually, a search for the city and other Yucatecan ruins was launched by John Lloyd Stephens and Frederick Catherwood, an American and Englishman. Stephens and Catherwood captured European and Euro-American imaginations with their book *Incidents of Travel in Yucatan* (1841), which came out just before the 1847 Caste War in the Yucatán. It was known for the intricate detail and great beauty of Catherwood's images of the ruins, which are sometimes still used by scholars who seek to understand details of the buildings that have eroded in the century and a half since publication[207]. This was the era of grand expeditions and public fascination with the concept of lost cities, and the book became a best-seller.

The area became inaccessible again at the start of the 1847 war and remained so until the war's conclusion in 1901, but this was soon followed up by the Mexican Revolution of 1910-1920. After the Revolution, the new Institutional Revolutionary Party (PRI) government established a different relationship with the Pre-Columbian past. This government was staunchly nationalist and viewed modern-day Mexico as a Mestizo state, a nation that was equally Spanish and indigenous in origin. Thus, Mexico's Pre-Columbian ruins were transformed from being crumbling heathen relics, which for centuries were considered best left to looters and the dead, into a source of pride and identity for the nation. At Chichén Itzá, this new interest took the form of a flurry of archaeological excavation and a major government-sponsored restoration of the jungle-covered El Castillo pyramid, with a parallel restoration of the nearby Temple of Warriors by the U.S.-based Carnegie Institution, both during the 1920s and 30s. This was followed in the 1930s by another government-sponsored excavation, this time into the side of the Castillo. That excavation discovered the two earlier pyramids buried under its surface. Excavations and restorations have continued in the decades since then, including impressive dredging of the Sacred Cenote in the 1950s[208].

---

207   "Frederick Catherwood's Lithographs" accessed online at: http://www.casa-catherwood.com/catherwoodinenglish.html

208   *Metals from the Cenote of Sacrifice: Chichen Itza, Yucatan* by S.K. Lothrop (1952). The Cambridge Museum.

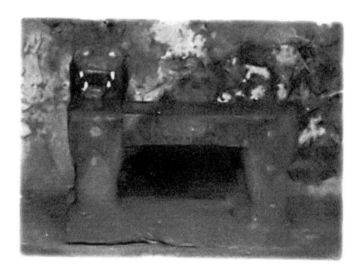

Photo of a throne depicting a jaguar, found inside El Castillo

Chichén Itzá is currently protected and managed under a 1972 law whose name translates in English as *"Federal Law on Monuments and Archaeological, Artistic and Historic Zones."* Under the provisions of that statute, the president declared the ruins an "archaeological monument" in 1986, which places the site under the management of the National Institute of Anthropology and History (INAH) based in Mexico City. In 1987, the state of Yucatan - where the ruins are located - created its own unique Board of Units of Cultural and Tourism Services, which oversees the conservation and touristic promotion of all of the major archaeological sites within the region.[209]

Chichén Itzá received further recognition in 1988 when Mexico requested its inscription on the list of World Heritage Sites. This list, which includes the Taj Mahal and the royal palace at Versailles, catalogues the most significant locations in world history and culture, as well as the Earth's most precious natural locations. The significance of the site for the Mexican people is indicated by the fact that it was part of only the second group of sites submitted by their government for inscription.[210]

This promotion, aided by the site's photogenic ruins, has led to Chichén Itzá becoming one of the region's premier tourist sites, attracting between 3,500-8,000 visitors a day. In fact, the splendor of El Castillo has made it a stand-in for the entire nation of Mexico in tourism campaigns for years. However, the affection for Chichén Itzá is not something simply manufactured for tourism either, as it

209   "Pre-Hispanic City of Chichen Itza" at the UNESCO World Heritage List, accessed online at:
       http://whc.unesco.org/en/list/483
210   "Pre-Hispanic City of Chichen Itza" at the UNESCO World Heritage List, accessed online at:
       http://whc.unesco.org/en/list/483

has long since become a point of Mexican pride since the 1920 revolution. The depth of this feeling was seen in 2007, when the "New7Wonders" Foundation began an international contest in which the public was invited to vote on a new list of "Seven Wonders of the World." All of the winners achieved their status in part through a public (typically government-sponsored) campaign, and Mexicans voted in droves for Chichén Itzá, putting it ahead of Mexico's other impressive ruins[211].

Ironically, it is this love that is today the greatest threat to the conservation of the site. While made of stone, much of the structure of the buildings is reconstructed and relatively fragile when under stress. In 2006, tourists were no longer allowed to climb the Castillo, and in 2011 INAH asked for the increased number of visitors coming to view the shadows move on the Castillo on the equinox to remain off of all of the structures and avoid other activities that have the potential to damage the site[212].

Another threat comes from the increasing presence of acid rain in the region. The reason why elaborate carvings survived to be recorded by Frederick Catherwood in the 19th century yet decomposed so quickly in the late 19th and early 20th centuries is largely due to the increased acidity in the rainfall throughout the Yucatán Peninsula. Since the structures are built of limestone (like the Peninsula itself), they are particularly susceptible to erosion, and an increasing amount of detail has permanently disappeared from the buildings' facades. For instance, by the late 1980s, a black crust of acid deposit covered an entire wall of the Grand Ballcourt in the city[213].

The final challenge facing the ruins currently is a growing conflict over who controls the ruins. After the Mexican Revolution, the government - along with the majority of Mestizos in central Mexico - came to view the ancient ruins as an example of shared national patrimony to be protected by the central state. However, the local Maya have increasingly asserted that these sites were not created by the ancestors of the Mestizos (who, if they have indigenous ancestry, tend to be from groups like the Aztec from central Mexico) but instead by their ancestors. While INAH recognizes this special relationship in a small way by allowing Maya to enter the ruins without paying fees, the locals push for greater benefits. At Chichén Itzá, this has created a conflict over whether, how many and where Maya artisans can sell their handicrafts to tourists, and this reached a head in 2006 when Subcomandante Marcos, the spokesman of the Zapatista revolutionary group (EZLN), came to Chichén Itzá. The EZLN represents Mayan communities in the state of Chiapas who had reached out to their Yucatecan cousins and sent Marcos to the state of Yucatán. The fact that the site remains potent enough that a world-renowned Mayan revolutionary will visit over a debate regarding vendors' rights is evidence of the increasingly contested nature of this particular space[214].

211   "Chichen Itza among New 7 Wonders of the World" by Suzanne Barbezat. Accessed online at:
       http://gomexico.about.com/b/2007/07/09/chichen-itza-among-new-7-wonders-of-the-world.htm
212   "Mexican Pyramids Under Threat from Equinox Revellers" by Robin Yapp for *The Telegraph* accessed online at:
       http://www.telegraph.co.uk/news/worldnews/centralamericaandthecaribbean/mexico/8390686/Mexican-pyramids-under-threat-from-Equinox-revellers.html
213   "New Threat to Maya Ruins: Acid Rain" by John Noble Wilford, for the *New York Times* Aug 8, 1989. Accessed online at :http://www.nytimes.com/1989/08/08/science/new-threat-to-maya-ruins-acid-rain.html?pagewanted=all&src=pm
214   "Marcos Rips Up Script: 'We're Going to Chichen Itzá" by Al Giordano Jan 20, 2006. Accessed online at:
       http://www.narconews.com/Issue40/article1570.html

Elaborately carved masks that show signs of weatherization

Thus stands Chichén Itzá at the dawn of the new millennium. It is a proud and ancient city, increasingly better understood by scholars (if not always the general public),but weathering around the edges. It also stands squarely within the crosshairs of a struggle over the patrimony of Mexico, a debate that reverberates around the world as indigenous peoples and national governments grapple over control, interpretation and profit of heritage sites.

With such a wealth of archaeological sites available in the Mayan heartland, Mayapán took a back seat to more famous sites like Tikal, Calakmul, Uxmal and Chichén Itzá, but the first serious archaeological work at the site was conducted in 1938 by Ralph T. Patton for the Carnegie Institution. This was followed up by a number of other Carnegie expeditions after World War II, which served to map all of the major structures within the walls and do detailed examinations of the buildings of the central plaza.

While a number of archaeologists have examined these central buildings since that time, much of the city's ruins remain in the hands of private Mayan farmers who continue to work the land. It was not until 1996 that the Instituto Nacional de Antropologia y Historia (INAH) began restoring the site and making it widely available for tourism. Since the early 21st century, the site has once again become a center for important research, including the Proyecto los Fundamentos Ecónomico de Mayapán (Economic Fundamentals of Mayapán Project) out of the State University of New York at Albany[215].

These researchers have shown that the city was far more extensive and important than previous archaeologists had believed[216].

Online Resources

Bibliography

Andrews, Anthony P.; E. Wyllys Andrews V, and Fernando Robles Castellanos (January 2003). "The Northern Maya Collapse and its Aftermath". Ancient Mesoamerica (New York: Cambridge University Press)

Aveni, Anthony F. (1997). Stairways to the Stars: Skywatching in Three Great Ancient Cultures. New York: John Wiley & Sons.

Brunhouse, Robert (1971). Sylvanus Morley and the World of the Ancient Mayas. Norman, Oklahoma: University of Oklahoma Press.

Charnay, Désiré (1887). Ancient Cities of the New World: Being Voyages and Explorations in Mexico and Central America from 1857–1882. J. Gonino and Helen S. Conant (trans.). New York: Harper & Brothers.

Coe, Michael D. (1999). The Maya. Ancient peoples and places series (6th edition, fully revised and expanded ed.). London and New York: Thames & Hudson.

Coggins, Clemency Chase (1984). Cenote of Sacrifice: Maya Treasures from the Sacred Well at Chichén Itzá. Austin, TX: University of Texas Press.

Colas, Pierre R.; and Alexander Voss (2006). "A Game of Life and Death – The Maya Ball Game". In Nikolai Grube (ed.). Maya: Divine Kings of the Rain Forest. Eva Eggebrecht and Matthias Seidel (assistant eds.). Cologne, Germany: Könemann. pp. 186–191. ISBN 978-3-8331-1957-6. OCLC 71165439.

Demarest, Arthur (2004). Ancient Maya: The Rise and Fall of a Rainforest Civilization. Case Studies in Early Societies, No. 3. Cambridge: Cambridge University Press.

Miller, Mary Ellen (1999). Maya Art and Architecture. London and New York: Thames & Hudson.

Perry, Richard D. (ed.) (2001). Exploring Yucatan: A Traveler's Anthology. Santa Barbara, CA:

---

215   Homepage of the Proyecto los Fundamentos Económico de Mayapán (PEMY), accessed online at: http://www.albany.edu/mayapan/index.shtml

216   "Revisiting Mayapan: Mexico's Last Maya Capital" by Susan Milbrath and Carlos Peraza Lope (2003). In the Journal *Ancient Mesoamerica*. V 14(01) pg 1-46.

Espadaña Press.

Phillips, Charles (2006, 2007). The Complete Illustrated History of the Aztecs & Maya: The definitive chronicle of the ancient peoples of Central America & Mexico - including the Aztec, Maya, Olmec, Mixtec, Toltec & Zapotec. London: Anness Publishing Ltd. ISBN 1-84681-197-X. OCLC 642211652.

Schele, Linda; and David Freidel (1990). A Forest of Kings: The Untold Story of the Ancient Maya (Reprint ed.). New York: Harper Perennial.

Sharer, Robert J.; with Loa P. Traxler (2006). The Ancient Maya (6th (fully revised) ed.). Stanford, CA: Stanford University Press.

Thompson, J. Eric S. (1966). The Rise and Fall of Maya Civilization. Norman, Oklahoma: University of Oklahoma Press.

Berlin , Heinrich (April 1967). "The Destruction of Structure 5D-33-1st at Tikal". American Antiquity (Washington, D. C., USA: Society for American Archaeology) 32 (2): 241–242. ISSN 0002-7316. JSTOR 277915. OCLC 754651089. Retrieved 06-05-13. (subscription required)

Coe, Michael D. (1999). The Maya. Ancient peoples and places series (6th edition, fully revised and expanded ed.). London and New York: Thames & Hudson. ISBN 0-500-28066-5.

Drew, David (1999). The Lost Chronicles of the Mayan Kings. Los Angeles: University of California Press.

Gill, Richardson B. (2000). The Great Maya Droughts: Water, Life, and Death. Albuquerque: University of New Mexico Press. ISBN 0-8263-2194-1. OCLC 43567384.

Harrison, Peter D. (2006). "Maya Architecture at Tikal". In Nikolai Grube (ed.). Maya: Divine Kings of the Rain Forest. Eva Eggebrecht and Matthias Seidel (assistant eds.). Köln: Könemann. pp. 218–231. ISBN 3-8331-1957-8. OCLC 71165439.

Jones, Grant D. (1998). The Conquest of the Last Maya Kingdom. Stanford, California, USA: Stanford University Press. ISBN 9780804735223. OCLC 38747674.

Kelly, Joyce (1996). An Archaeological Guide to Northern Central America: Belize, Guatemala, Honduras, and El Salvador. Norman: University of Oklahoma Press. ISBN 0-8061-2858-5. OCLC 34658843.

Looper, Matthew G. (1999). "New Perspectives on the Late Classic Political History of Quirigua, Guatemala". Ancient Mesoamerica (Cambridge and New York: Cambridge University Press) 10 (2): 263–280. doi:10.1017/S0956536199101135. ISSN 0956-5361. OCLC 86542758.

Looper, Matthew G. (2003). Lightning Warrior: Maya Art and Kingship at Quirigua. Linda Schele series in Maya and pre-Columbian studies. Austin: University of Texas Press. ISBN 0-292-70556-5. OCLC 52208614.

Martin, Simon; and Nikolai Grube (2000). Chronicle of the Maya Kings and Queens: Deciphering the Dynasties of the Ancient Maya. London and New York: Thames & Hudson. ISBN 0-500-05103-8. OCLC 47358325.

Martin, Simon; and Nikolai Grube (2008). Chronicle of the Maya Kings and Queens: Deciphering the Dynasties of the Ancient Maya (2nd (revised) ed.). London and New York: Thames & Hudson. ISBN 978-0-500-28726-2. OCLC 191753193.

Miller, Mary Ellen (1999). Maya Art and Architecture. London and New York: Thames & Hudson. ISBN 0-500-20327-X. OCLC 41659173.

Miller, Mary; and Karl Taube (1993). The Gods and Symbols of Ancient Mexico and the Maya: An Illustrated Dictionary of Mesoamerican Religion. London: Thames & Hudson. ISBN 0-500-05068-6. OCLC 27667317.

Schele, Linda; and Peter Mathews (1999). The Code of Kings: The language of seven Maya temples and tombs. New York: Simon & Schuster. ISBN 978-0-684-85209-6. OCLC 41423034.

Sharer, Robert J.; with Loa P. Traxler (2006). The Ancient Maya (6th, fully revised ed.). Stanford, CA: Stanford University Press. ISBN 0-8047-4817-9. OCLC 57577446.

Webster, David L. (2002). The Fall of the Ancient Maya: Solving the Mystery of the Maya Collapse. London: Thames & Hudson. ISBN 0-500-05113-5. OCLC 48753878.

Free Books by Charles River Editors

We have brand new titles available for free most days of the week. To see which of our titles are currently free, click on this link.

Discounted Books by Charles River Editors

We have titles at a discount price of just 99 cents everyday. To see which of our titles are currently 99 cents, click on this link.

38346719R00077

Printed in Great Britain
by Amazon